MW01680036

While every precaution has been
publisher assumes no responsibili
resulting from the use of the information contained herein.

LIVING WITH MINIMALIST INTERIOR DESIGN STYLE

First edition. July 3, 2023.

Copyright © 2023 Adil Masood Qazi.

ISBN: 979-8223285557

Written by Adil Masood Qazi.

Also by Adil Masood Qazi

Writing

Writing Nonfiction and Fiction Book for Beginners

Standalone

Beginners Book of Home Decorating and Interior Design
Interior Styles
Interior Design: An Introduction
Interior Design - A Comprehensive Introduction Guide
Starting an Interior Design Business
Introduction to Entrepreneur Thinking
A Guide To Mastering The Art of Your Thoughts and Emotions
Introduction to Sustainable Interior Design
How Interior Designers Think
Design Your Dream: A Guide to Furniture and Decor Selection
How not to Fail in Business
Ergonomics in Home
How Interior Designers Get Ideas
Ultimate Guide to Understanding Soft Skills for Interior Designers
Introduction to Classic Interior Style
Living with Minimalist Interior Design Style
Living With African Interior Design Style

Table of Contents

About the Author

Adil Masood Qazi is a highly accomplished interior designer and esteemed educator with a passion for transforming spaces. With a master's degree in Interior Design and an impressive 28 years of professional experience, Adil has spearheaded numerous residential and commercial projects, leaving an indelible mark on the industry. His keen eye for aesthetics, meticulous attention to detail, and innovative design solutions have earned him widespread recognition. Alongside his design career, Adil is an esteemed educationist, boasting 25 years of teaching experience in interior design. He is dedicated to imparting knowledge, nurturing aspiring designers, and shaping the future of the field through his mentorship and expertise."

LIVING
WITH
MINIMALIST
INTERIOR DESIGN
STYLE
Adil Masood Qazi

Introduction to Minimalist Interior Design

What is Minimalism?

Simplicity, functionality, and intentionality are values embraced by minimalism, a design philosophy and way of life. Removing extraneous items and concentrating on what really matters is a choice. The fundamental goal of minimalism is to design places that are tidy, uncluttered, and devoid of pointless distractions.

Clean lines, neutral colour schemes, and a lack of intricate or overbearing embellishments are characteristics of minimalism in interior design. The intention is to instill a sense of peace and tranquilly, allowing the environment to breathe and the mind to unwind. It's all about striking a pleasing balance between form and purpose.

The aesthetics of a space are only one aspect of minimalism. It also includes a manner of thinking and living. It promotes taking an intentional and considerate attitude to the things we own, the things we do, and the connections we foster. It nudges us to let go of the pointless and put our attention on what is actually valuable and enjoyable.

Simplicity is one of the main characteristics of minimalism. It entails reducing to the bare minimum, getting rid of extras, and adopting a more organised strategy. This can be done by carefully selecting the furnishings and artefacts in a room, making sure that each one has a function and adds to the beauty.

Functionality is a key component of minimalism. Every component of a minimalist design has a purpose and a defined function. Furniture is picked out based on its usefulness, and multi-purpose pieces are frequently preferred to maximise space efficiency. This focus on practicality encourages clarity and a sense of purpose in the design.

Neutral colours like white, grey, and earth tones are also heavily emphasised in minimalism. These hues evoke a feeling of peace and tranquilly, which helps the mind unwind and the eye concentrate on the room's shape and texture. They offer a timeless setting that is simple to modify to suit shifting fashions or individual tastes.

In addition to its aesthetic benefits, minimalism promotes deliberate consumption and choice-making. It makes us reevaluate our spending patterns, think about how our decisions may affect the environment, and value experiences over material goods. We can decrease waste, save money, and live more sustainably if we adopt a minimalist mindset.

It is not necessary to live a life of deprivation or in a stark setting to be minimalist. Finding the right mix between simplicity and comfort is important, as is designing areas that express our ideals and objectives. It's about encouraging serenity and tranquilly in a world that can sometimes feel chaotic.

In short, minimalism is a way of life rather than just a design aesthetic. It provides a novel approach to interior design, emphasising simplicity, use, and deliberate living. We can design places that are not only aesthetically beautiful but also encourage a sense of calm and well-being by embracing simplicity. It's a call to purge the unnecessary and concentrate on what really counts, both in our immediate surroundings and across our entire lives.

The Philosophy of Minimalist Design

In addition to being aesthetically pleasing, the minimalist design philosophy attempts to simplify and get rid of the superfluous in all aspects of life. Minimalist design is fundamentally about embracing the essential qualities of a space, object, or experience and eliminating any extraneous features that obscure those qualities.

A purposeful and conscious approach to design, where each choice is carefully evaluated, is encouraged by minimalism. It contests the idea that more is better and places an emphasis on the benefits of less. It marks a break from excess and consumerism culture and invites us to pay attention to what really matters and find beauty in simplicity.

The creation of clear, distraction-free spaces is one of the fundamental tenets of minimalist design. This entails curating the furniture and accessories in a room with care, making sure that each piece has a function and adds to the aesthetic of the room as a whole. Minimalist design encourages quiet and serenity by removing unnecessary visual distractions, which frees the mind to concentrate and enjoy the beauty of the essential components.

Additionally, usefulness is embraced by minimalism, where each component of a design has a useful function. Furniture is picked for its practicality and comfort, and extraneous decorations are removed. This focus on utility improves a space's usability while also bringing out its efficiency and clarity.

Clean lines and a neutral colour scheme are frequently included in minimalism in addition to simplicity and functionality. While neutral hues like whites, greys, and earth tones offer a timeless and calming backdrop, straight lines and geometric patterns generate a sense of order and harmony. These design decisions highlight the inherent beauty of items and materials by emphasising their form and texture.

Beyond actual locations and items, the minimalist design ethos also affects our way of life and consumption patterns. Making deliberate decisions about the things we bring into our lives is encouraged by minimalism, which challenges our inclinations towards consumerism. It encourages us to prioritise quality over quantity and invest in well-made, long-lasting products rather than accumulating a large number of disposable possessions.

By minimising waste and taking into account how our decisions will affect the environment, minimalist design also promotes sustainable practises. We can reduce our carbon footprint and help create a more environmentally friendly future by embracing minimalism. This way of thinking encourages a change from a disposable society to one that prioritises enduring quality and thoughtful consumption.

In addition to its aesthetic benefits, minimalist design encourages mindfulness and intentionality. It encourages us to take our time, enjoy the moment, and find joy in life's little pleasures. We make room for clarity and attention by clearing our mental and physical areas. A more meaningful and rewarding life can be had by prioritising experiences, connections, and personal development over material stuff.

Finally, the minimalist design ethos is founded on the idea that less is more. It embraces functionality, purpose, and simplicity in an effort to design meaningful and necessary environments and experiences. By adopting a minimalist perspective, we may clear our mental and physical spaces of clutter, lessen distractions, and concentrate on the things that genuinely make us happy and fulfilled. Finding the ideal harmony between simplicity and refinement is what minimalism is all about—not giving up comfort or beauty. It is a call to live more purposefully, mindfully, and with an appreciation for the beauty of the fundamentals.

Benefits of Minimalist Living

MINIMALIST LIVING HAS arisen as a revitalising option that has many advantages to those who choose to adopt it in today's fast-paced and consumer-driven world. It is a deliberate way of living that encourages people to live simply, declutter their surroundings, and pay attention to what really matters. People can gain a variety of benefits that extend well beyond the physical world by purposefully cutting out the excess and adopting a minimalist lifestyle.

The sensation of freedom that minimalist living fosters is one of its main advantages. People can free up both physical and emotional space by letting rid of pointless commitments and goods. A more organised existence and a clearer mind are made possible by the decluttering and organising process. Opportunities for personal development, creativity, and discovery arise from this newly discovered space and clarity. Individuals can pursue their hobbies, objectives, and dreams with a renewed sense of purpose and focus when they are less burdened by bodily and mental baggage.

Additionally, adopting a minimal lifestyle fosters a deeper sense of tranquilly and calm. People can create a quiet and serene environment by clearing away clutter and keeping things simple. Reduced visual distractions in a clean environment promote relaxation and mental clarity. People can live lighter, more serene lives with fewer possessions to manage and preserve. This focus on mindfulness and simplicity fosters a state of inner tranquilly and contentment that can have a positive effect on general well-being.

Financial independence is a key benefit of living simply. Individuals can escape the cycle of materialism and excessive spending by adopting a minimalist lifestyle. Quality is more important to minimalists than quantity, and they choose to buy only what they truly need rather than mindlessly accumulating things. Individuals who take a deliberate approach to their spending can save money, pay off debt, and achieve financial security. By cutting out wasteful spending, people can put their money towards important connections, experiences, and personal development.

Sustainable living and environmental stewardship are further benefits of minimalist living. Minimalists lessen their environmental impact and contribute to a more sustainable future by spending less and making thoughtful decisions. They place a high value on items and materials that are long-lasting, environmentally friendly, and produced responsibly. Minimalists actively contribute to resource conservation and the protection of the environment by reducing waste and adopting the "less is more" philosophy.

Improved mental and emotional health is one advantage of minimalist living that is frequently disregarded. People can feel less stress and anxiety by simplifying their life. The mind might become overloaded and worn out by the constant barrage of knowledge, possessions, and obligations. By providing a break from the turmoil, minimalism enables people to concentrate on what genuinely makes them happy and fulfilled. It promotes a mental change away from relentlessly seeking approval from others and towards developing internal satisfaction and self-awareness.

Relationships grow deeper and more profound when people live simply. De-cluttering allows people to devote more time and effort to strengthening relationships with their loved ones. Minimalism promotes spending quality time with loved ones and friends, allowing for more dialogue, shared experiences, and sincere bonds. Minimalists cultivate a vibrant and rewarding social life by putting relationships above material goods.

In conclusion, living a minimalist lifestyle has a wealth of advantages that go beyond material gain. Individuals can feel more freedom, calm, and contentment by simplifying their life. Adopting a minimalist lifestyle has many benefits, including improved relationships, sustainability, financial freedom, and enhanced mental health. People can design a life that is purposeful, meaningful, and fulfilling by purposefully cutting out the superfluous and concentrating on what really counts. Minimalism is about actively choosing a simpler, more intentional way of living that is in line with one's ideals and results in a higher sense of joy and harmony rather than about deprivation or sacrifice.

Understanding the Principles of Minimalism

Simplicity and Clutter-Free Spaces

The idea of simplicity and clutter-free places has drawn a lot of attention in today's fast-paced and cluttered world. Many people are adopting the minimalist lifestyle and choosing to live in a space that is more streamlined and organised. This tendency towards simplicity is not merely a fad; it has many positive effects on our physical, mental, and emotional health.

The sense of quiet and tranquilly that simplicity in our living environments fosters is one of its main benefits. Our thoughts might feel clear and focused when our surroundings are uncluttered of extraneous items. Because there is less clutter around, we may unwind and feel peaceful without being interrupted. When we simplify our environment, finding tranquilly and relishing periods of isolation become simpler.

Efficiency and productivity are also enhanced by simplicity. It is simpler to find and reach the things we need when our physical spaces are clutter-free. By not having to look through mountains of possessions, we can save precious time and energy. This effectiveness goes beyond our immediate surroundings and can have a favourable effect on our daily jobs and routines. We can concentrate our attention on the tasks that really matter and advance towards our goals with less distractions and visual clutter.

Our mental and emotional health can benefit from a minimalist approach to our living spaces as well. It has been discovered that clutter increases feelings of tension and worry. A sensation of overwhelm and difficulty finding peace of mind might result from having too many things in our living environments. Contrarily, simplifying our environment can produce a sensation of freedom and lightness, lowering stress levels and encouraging a more optimistic outlook.

Our physical health can be enhanced by simple and clutter-free environments in addition to the emotional advantages. Spaces that are cluttered are harder to keep clean and maintain, which can cause dust, allergens, and even mould to build up. We may create a healthier living environment by reducing the amount of possessions we own and by keeping our places tidy and organised. It becomes simpler to keep things clean and make sure there is enough ventilation, which might be beneficial for our respiratory health.

Additionally, simplicity and clutter-free environments promote responsible consumption. In a society where consumption is king, adopting a minimalist lifestyle enables us to make more thoughtful purchasing decisions. We become more conscious of our necessities versus wants and put our attention on collecting things that will actually improve our life. By cutting back on wasteful purchases, we support sustainability initiatives and lessen our environmental effect.

It is crucial to remember that minimalism and simplicity do not imply a lack of individuality or self-expression. Instead, a minimalist style of design and living encourages deliberate and considerate decisions. It inspires us to fill our spaces with things that are meaningful to us and make us happy. Instead than just acquiring goods for the sake of it, each object might be carefully chosen and valued for its quality and meaning.

Numerous advantages that go beyond our physical environment are provided by simple and clutter-free environments. They encourage serenity, boost output, improve mental and emotional health, and support a better and more sustainable way of life. We can design areas that reflect our ideals and serve as havens from the craziness of the outside world by embracing minimalism. So let's aim for simplicity and appreciate the beauty of a life devoid of clutter.

Functionality and Practicality

PRACTICALITY AND MINIMALIST functionality have emerged as driving concepts in interior design for producing environments that are both aesthetically pleasing and extremely functional. As a design concept, minimalism prioritises clarity, simplicity, and a focus on fundamental components. Functionality is prioritised over obtrusive ornamentation in an effort to create environments that are effective, useful, and meaningful.

Focusing on functional design with a minimal aesthetic is one of its main components. Every component of a minimalist interior has a purpose and was carefully picked. Furniture is chosen for its usefulness and functionality, making sure that it not only looks attractive but also offers comfort and usability. A sleek, streamlined sofa with clear lines that is intended to provide comfortable seating without needless frills or excessive ornamentation, for instance, might be found in a minimalist living room.

THE DESIGN AND ARRANGEMENT of spaces can also be minimalistically useful. The emphasis of the design is on producing functional floor designs that make the best use of the available space. The placement of furniture and other items is designed to make things accessible and easy to move around. This strategy is especially useful in compact areas where every square inch matters. Minimalist design contributes to the open, airy, and large feeling by focusing on practicality and reducing clutter.

Another essential component of minimalist design is utility. It entails picking useful, enduring, and simple to maintain materials, finishes, and furnishings. For instance, you might discover slender, minimalistic cabinets in a minimalist kitchen built of premium materials that are durable. In a similar vein, practical flooring options might be prioritised, such as easily cleanable surfaces that are also aesthetically pleasing and useful.

Storage options can also be functionally minimalist. Storage is frequently effectively incorporated into the design of a minimalist environment to reduce visual clutter. Furniture with several uses, hidden storage, and built-in storage are typical elements of minimalist design. These components offer plenty of storage space for daily goods while maintaining a tidy and organised appearance. Minimalist design promotes a clutter-free atmosphere by putting an emphasis on useful storage options, which improves the room's overall practicality and usability.

The guiding premise of minimalist functioning is the idea that "less is more." This way of thinking promotes eliminating extraneous components and concentrating on what matters most. Minimalist design creates areas that are uncluttered and distraction-free by embracing simplicity and focusing on the fundamentals. This method encourages peace and tranquilly, enabling the mind to concentrate on the task at hand or to simply take in the beauty of the environment.

Additionally, simple functionality encourages responsible consumption and sustainability. Minimalist design minimises waste and promotes responsible consumption by utilising strong, long-lasting materials and furnishings, as well as by minimising excess and pointless adornment. It adheres to the fundamentals of sustainable living by valuing quality above quantity and promoting deliberate, deliberate choices.

Modern home design is fundamentally about practicality and basic functionality. Minimalist interiors establish a harmonic balance between beauty and usefulness by putting an emphasis on meaningful design, effective layouts, useful materials, and creative storage solutions. This method improves functionality, comfort, and general well-being in addition to producing spaces that are aesthetically pleasing. We can design environments that are not just beautiful but also very functional and purposeful by embracing minimalism and its emphasis on functionality.

Embracing Minimalist Aesthetics

FOR INDIVIDUALS LOOKING for a tidy, contemporary, and aesthetically pleasant living space, adopting minimalist aesthetics has become a popular choice in the world of interior design. As a design concept, minimalism emphasises simplicity, purity, and the removal of extraneous features. It honours the elegance of simple shapes, wide open areas, and subdued colour schemes.

The emphasis on clarity and simplicity is one of the main characteristics of minimalist design. Less is more is embraced in minimalist design, which favours clear lines and uncluttered areas. It stays away from too ornate, detailed detailing, and extraneous frills. Instead, it emphasises the beauty of simplicity by employing the fewest possible design components to provide a great visual effect. Each component can shine and be valued in its own right thanks to the simplified design.

Open and roomy layouts are also prioritised in minimalist design. Minimalist interior design fosters a feeling of freedom and openness in a space by removing extraneous furnishings and accents. This not only improves the aesthetic appeal but also fosters a pleasant and serene atmosphere. The absence of clutter creates a calm and quiet environment by allowing the sight and mind to rest.

Neutral colours and earthy hues are popular choices for the minimalist aesthetic's colour pallet. The minimalist colour scheme is dominated by shades of white, grey, beige, and muted colours. This colour scheme heightens a space's impression of harmony and simplicity. The ageless and opulent appearance of minimalist design is achieved by employing a limited colour pallet.

The emphasis on natural light is another component of minimalist design. Large windows and open floor plans are frequently used in minimalist interiors to increase the amount of natural light. This not only improves the space's overall ambiance but also fosters a sense of connection with the outside. The minimalist design is elevated by natural light, which also gives the room a sense of warmth, brightness, and life.

Minimalist aesthetics pay attention to textures and materials in addition to colour scheme and natural light. Smooth surfaces, such as polished concrete, glass, or sleek metals, are frequently used in minimalist design to convey an air of elegance and sex. Natural elements, such as wood or stone, give the minimalist area a cosy, organic feel. The contrast of various textures gives the aesthetic's overall depth and visual intrigue.

Choosing furniture and accessories in accordance with minimalist aesthetics is another aspect of interior design. Functional furniture with clear lines and a streamlined style is preferred in minimalist rooms. Furniture is frequently chosen for its simplicity and functionality, placing an emphasis on usability and comfort over pointless decoration. The number of decorative things is kept to a minimum, and each one is carefully chosen to blend in with the general style and add to the visual harmony of the room.

Overall, there are many advantages to adopting minimalist aesthetics in home design. It produces settings that are ageless, calm, and visually appealing. A sense of serenity and tranquilly is facilitated by the clarity and simplicity of minimalist design.

The open floor plans and muted colour scheme give the impression of freedom and space. Minimalist design fosters a greater awareness of each distinct aspect in a room by removing extraneous components and putting the emphasis on crucial ones. A living area that embraces minimalist aesthetics can become a haven of peace and beauty, offering a place for rest, reflection, and a connection with the spirit of design itself.

Creating a Minimalist Color Palette

Neutral Color Schemes in Minimalist Interior

A basic component of minimalist interior design, neutral colour palettes are essential for establishing a calm, peaceful, and balanced living environment. In minimalist design, the use of neutral colours creates a clear and uncluttered visual approach that emphasises simplicity and lets other design components take centre stage.

The core of minimalist design is neutral hues like whites, greys, beiges, and soft tones. These hues were selected for their capacity to promote serenity as well as their classic and adaptability. Minimalist interiors produce a visually cohesive and unified effect that is both calming and elegant by utilising neutral colour combinations.

One of the main benefits of neutral colour schemes is their capacity to impart an airy, roomy feeling to a room. Lighter neutral colours, like white and light grey, reflect natural light, giving the room the appearance of being bigger and brighter. This improves the space's ambience overall, giving it a light and welcoming sense. By facilitating smooth transitions between various regions of the room, the choice of neutral colours also helps to create a sense of continuity and flow.

In minimalist homes, the use of neutral colour palettes creates a background on which other design elements can stand out. A muted colour scheme draws attention to other important design elements including furniture, architectural details, and artwork. This enables these components to stand out and be seen. Backgrounds made of neutral colours let the eye relax and focus on the room's attractiveness without being distracted.

Neutral colour choices also provide a great degree of adaptability and flexibility. They act as a timeless base that is simple to modify to shifting fashion trends and individual tastes. Because they are not constrained by particular fashions or fads, neutral colours are a reliable and long-lasting option for minimalist interiors. They produce an air of sophistication and timelessness that can be savoured for years to come.

The capacity of neutral colour palettes to produce a feeling of tranquilly and peace is another benefit. Neutral colours frequently conjure up images of nature and emotions of serenity. These hues have a calming influence on the psyche and can aid in fostering a stress-free and comfortable atmosphere. Neutral colours contribute to the overall feeling of balance and harmony in a minimalist design, where clarity and simplicity are key.

It's crucial to take texture and contrast into account when utilising neutral colour palettes in minimalist decor. The utilisation of various textures and materials becomes even more important because the colour palette is more muted. Natural materials like wood, stone, or textured fabrics can be added to a space to provide depth and aesthetic appeal. This makes the design haptic and keeps it from feeling flat or repetitive.

A crucial element of minimalist interior design, neutral colour palettes add to the general tranquilly, simplicity, and visual cohesiveness of the space. The choice of neutral hues produces a peaceful background that lets other design components stand out and be bold. Additionally, neutral hues encourage a feeling of openness and space, which makes the space appear lighter and bigger. They are a fantastic option for individuals looking for a minimalist design that will stand the test of time due to their adaptability and timeless appeal.

Minimalist interiors may create a calming and welcoming ambiance that encourages relaxation and a sense of well-being by incorporating neutral colour palettes.

Accent Colors and Contrasts in Minimalist Interior

THE THOUGHTFUL USE of accent colours and contrasts can have a significant impact on the overall aesthetic and visual appeal of a room, especially in the field of minimalist interior design, where simplicity and restraint are paramount. Although neutral colour palettes predominate in minimalist homes, adding deliberate contrasts and accent colours may give the space life, personality, and visual intrigue.

In minimalist homes, accent colours act as focus points to highlight certain nooks, crannies, or architectural details. They add a feeling of visual interest and produce brief contrasts with the largely neutral colour scheme. Accent colours may make a strong statement and give depth to the overall design when used sparingly and intelligently.

It's crucial to choose hues that blend in with the overall aesthetic and complement the existing colour scheme when choosing accent colours for minimalist interiors. Choosing hues that are either similar to or complementary to the neutral tones results in a uniform and well-balanced appearance. For instance, a splash of vivid yellow can instantly invigorate the room and serve as a focal point when placed against a background of soothing greys and whites.

In minimalist interior design, contrasts are crucial, both in terms of colour and texture. They add visual interest and keep the area from appearing dull or monotonous. Different design components, such as furniture, accessories, artwork, or architectural aspects, can be used to introduce contrasting elements.

Utilising hues that contrast one another on the colour wheel will produce contrasted colours. For instance, contrasting a warm, earthy colour like terracotta with a deep blue hue provides visual drama and depth to the room. Additionally, opposing textures can produce a tactile difference that adds visual interest and complexity to the design, such as smooth surfaces against rough textures or matte finishes against shiny surfaces.

Maintaining a sense of balance and restraint is essential when using accent colours and contrasts in minimalist homes. The objective is to produce moments of impact without detracting too much from the minimalist look as a whole. The design maintains cohesion and its simplicity and beauty by thoughtfully choosing the location and strength of accent colours and contrasts.

Additionally, accent hues and contrasts can be intentionally used to draw attention to particular architectural details or furniture in a room. For instance, a bold red accent wall might highlight a well constructed piece of furniture or a striking piece of art, establishing a focal point that grounds the space.

Accent colours and contrasts in minimalist decor can enhance the emotional ambiance of the room in addition to creating visual interest. Cool, calming tones can promote tranquilly, while warm, energetic hues can arouse excitement and vigour. Accent colours can be chosen to support and enhance the intended emotional experience by taking into account the desired mood and atmosphere of the place.

In minimalist interior design, accent colours and contrasts are used to give the room depth, visual interest, and individuality. Accent colours establish focal points and bring attention to particular regions or items when they are carefully chosen and used, whereas contrasts create visual curiosity and prevent monotony. Minimalist interiors can achieve a dynamic and engaging look that supports the overarching design concept by adding accent colours and contrasts with balance and moderation. The distinctiveness and character of the room are enhanced by these thoughtful design decisions, which also produce a calming and harmonious atmosphere.

Using Texture and Material to Add Depth in Minimalist Interiors

STRATEGIC USE OF TEXTURE and materials is essential in minimalist home design, where brevity and clean lines take centre stage, to add depth and aesthetic intrigue. Even while minimalism frequently emphasises a simple appearance, using various textures and materials can provide the room a physical and sensual experience.

Texture is the term used to describe how something looks on the outside. You may add a sense of richness, contrast, and visual curiosity to a minimalist space by incorporating different textures. Without affecting the design's general simplicity, it adds a layer of intricacy.

Natural materials are one method to add texture to minimalist spaces. Natural fibres, wood, and stone all provide warmth and organic charm to a space. The roughness of exposed brick walls, the softness of a natural fibre rug, or the grain of a wooden table may all produce a tactile experience that stimulates the senses and adds dimension to the design.

Additionally, blending several textures might result in a composition that is aesthetically lively and well-balanced. A contrast that increases the visual interest of the area is produced by blending smooth surfaces with rough textures, such as a sleek glass tables with a rough, textured wall. The contrast of textures draws the eye and adds depth while generating visual tension.

A minimalist interior's overall look is greatly influenced by the material choices made. Design can be improved and a sense of luxury and refinement can be created by choosing high-quality materials with rich textures and subtle differences. A leather sofa with its plush texture or a marble countertop with its distinctive veining, for instance, offer a touch of refinement and elegance to the room.

The use of monochromatic or restricted colour palettes is typical in minimalist interiors. In order to create visual interest and keep the area from feeling flat or one-dimensional, texture becomes even more important. The uniformity of the colour scheme is broken up with textured materials, such as woven fabrics, knitted blankets, or patterned tiles, which also help to establish a focal point within the design.

Adding texture can also be accomplished by utilising textiles like carpets, cushions, and curtains. While patterned or textured textiles provide personality and aesthetic interest, soft, velvety fabrics create a cosy and welcoming atmosphere. You can add depth and complexity to a minimalist environment while still keeping it tidy and uncluttered by layering various materials.

Maintaining a feeling of harmony and balance is crucial when introducing texture and materials into minimalist spaces. The objective is to provide a unified design that exudes intentionality and curation. A space can become cluttered and lose its minimalist appearance if there are too many competing textures or materials.

In order to emphasise the space's texture and materials, lighting is also quite important. You can emphasise the texture and provide lovely plays of light and shadow by placing light fixtures strategically and using various lighting techniques. It increases the design's depth and dimension and heightens the visual impact overall.

Finally, adding texture and materials to minimalist interiors gives the room a sense of depth, visual intrigue, and sensory experience. You may produce a rich and dynamic design that goes beyond the simplicity of minimalism by utilising a variety of textures and high-quality materials. An environment that is aesthetically appealing and engaging is produced by the thoughtful selection and ad hoc juxtaposition of textures and materials.

Essential Elements of Minimalist Furniture

Clean Lines and Geometric Shapes

Clean lines and geometric shapes characterise minimalist furniture design, which makes it a popular option for people looking for a straightforward yet elegant aesthetic in their living spaces. In order to promote peace and tranquilly, this design concept eliminates superfluous decoration and concentrates on the fundamentals of form and function.

The simplicity of minimalist furniture is one of its distinguishing features. Every component of the design has a purpose and has been carefully chosen to create a unified and harmonious appearance. This design is characterised by straight lines, acute angles, and geometric shapes, which add to the tidy and uncluttered appearance of minimalist furniture.

Clean lines and minimalist furniture give the room a feeling of balance and order. The absence of decorative decorations, whether on a sleek sofa, a streamlined coffee table, or a simple dining chair, draws attention to the basic shapes and proportions of the furniture. This form's simplicity is both aesthetically beautiful and practical because it encourages calm and lessens visual noise in the space.

Another important characteristic of minimalist furniture is geometric shapes. These shapes, which range from circular pendant lights to square and rectangular bookcases, give the design a feeling of structure and sophistication. The area is balanced and visually appealing because of the symmetry and order that geometric patterns and forms bring to it.

Less is more in minimalist furniture design. The furniture pieces become ageless and adaptable by removing superfluous details and concentrating on key ones. Because of this strategy, minimalist furniture may be easily incorporated into a wide range of interior design aesthetics, from contemporary to Scandinavian and everything in between.

The adaptability and versatility of minimalist furniture is one of its key benefits. It may effortlessly match various interior design trends thanks to its subtle and straightforward design. Modern, industrial, or historic homes can all benefit from the addition of minimalist furniture to improve the appearance.

Furniture that has a minimalist aesthetic also has practical advantages. Cleaning and maintenance are simple because of the sleek lines and flat surfaces. The furniture is simpler to maintain looking clean and new without complicated embellishments that might gather dust and filth.

Additionally, minimalist furniture provides a feeling of openness and space in the space. It is perfect for tiny flats or rooms with limited square footage because of its minimalist and uncomplicated design, which optically enhances the available space.

Functionality is a key consideration in the design of minimal furniture. Each item is painstakingly made to serve its intended function without adding extraneous details. These pieces prioritise usability and comfort, whether it's a minimalist sofa with a streamlined form or a modern dining table with smooth corners.

Minimalist furniture is advantageous in terms of sustainability and environmental friendliness. These furniture items are made to last by putting an emphasis on quality and durability, which lowers the need for frequent replacements. Furthermore, they won't go out of style due to their timeless design, thereby extending their useful life.

It's crucial to think about the materials used in the building of minimalist furniture while choosing it. Choose sustainable, high-quality materials like solid wood, organic fabrics, and environmentally friendly finishes. These decisions support a healthier and greener house in addition to being in line with the minimalist philosophy.

Furniture with clean, geometric lines and minimalist aesthetics has several advantages for interior design. Its elegance and simplicity evoke a sense of calmness, and its versatility enables it to seamlessly integrate with a variety of interior design styles. Minimalist furniture upholds the tenets of less is more by putting a focus on efficiency and sustainability, making it a great option for individuals looking for timelessly beautiful design. Modern, contemporary, or eclectic interiors can all benefit from having minimalist furniture because it adds elegance to the room.

Minimalist Seating and Storage Solutions

THE ADAGE "LESS IS more" applies to more than simply the aesthetic when it comes to minimalist interior design. It also holds true for any furniture and storage options put to use in the area. While yet retaining a sense of flair and sophistication, minimalist seating and storage solutions are made to be useful, practical, and inconspicuous.

Focus is placed on simplicity and clean lines in minimalist seating. The emphasis is on designing comfortable sitting alternatives without needless adornments, whether it be in the form of streamlined sofas, minimalist armchairs, or understated benches and stools. Straight edges, sharp angles, and a streamlined shape are frequent aspects of the design. By avoiding bulky and excessive furniture pieces, this minimalist approach not only produces an aesthetically pleasing appearance but also helps to maximise the space that is already present.

The adaptability of minimalist seating is one of its advantages. It may easily fit into any interior style, whether it be contemporary, modern, or even historic because of the design's clarity and simplicity. As a blank canvas, minimalist seating lets you experiment with various accents and accessories to get your preferred design.

Comfort is given top priority in minimalist seating designs in addition to visual appeal. Although they may appear simple, they are made to offer ergonomic support and guarantee a comfortable sitting experience. To ensure comfort and lifespan, the emphasis is on high-quality materials, such as cushioning with the right amount of firmness and durability.

The same ideals of simplicity and functionality guide minimalist storage solutions. The goal of minimalist storage solutions is to organise and clear the area without drawing attention to themselves. To keep a neat and tidy appearance, built-in cabinets and covert storage spaces are frequently used. These options efficiently conceal items while maintaining the visual emphasis on the key components of the space.

Efficiency and accessibility are also given top priority in minimalist storage solutions. The design ensures that goods are well-organized and accessible by taking into account the practicalities of storage. By doing so, visual distractions are removed and a sense of serenity and order is fostered in the area.

Minimalist seating and storage options frequently use natural and high-quality materials for their materials and finishes. Common materials include wood, leather, and metal, which not only increase the furniture's toughness but also give the overall design an air of refinement. The colour scheme is typically neutral and subtle, which enables the furniture to meld perfectly with the surroundings.

The ability of minimalist storage and seating options to save space is another important feature. They are perfect for smaller living areas where maximising every square inch is crucial due to their sleek form and tiny proportions. The minimalist design philosophy enables effective use of space without compromising on design or usefulness.

Additionally, simple storage and seating options help the space feel airy and free-flowing. They provide the impression that the area is larger by keeping furniture and storage units simple and unobtrusive and by allowing for simple movement inside the space.

Finally, eco-friendly and sustainable concepts are in line with minimalist storage and seating options. They are made to last a long time and require fewer replacements because they are made using high-quality materials and craftsmanship. This strategy encourages a more sustainable way of life while also reducing trash.

Simple, practical, and stylish are the tenets that minimalist storage and seating solutions uphold. Their minimalist interior is unified by their simple lines, subtle design, and effective use of space. They add versatility, comfort, and a refined air to any living area, whether they are simple storage choices or seating options. They also support eco-friendly beliefs by putting an emphasis on high-quality products and sustainable practises. You may design a practical and aesthetically pleasing space that celebrates the beauty of simplicity with minimal seating and storage.

Quality and Durability in Furniture Choices

THE QUALITY AND LONGEVITY of the furniture selections are also important considerations in minimalist interior design, in addition to the aesthetics. Every piece of furniture in a minimalist setting should have a specific function and survive the test of time. When choosing furniture for a minimalist aesthetic, quality and durability are important considerations because they add to the overall lifetime and functionality of the room.

Furniture with a minimalistic aesthetic typically has a clear and straightforward design. The emphasis is on streamlined appearance, clean lines, and sparse decorations. This does not, however, imply sacrificing quality. In reality, the use of fine materials and craftsmanship is frequently emphasised in minimalist furniture.

Choose sturdy furniture for a minimalist space by choosing items with solid wood, metal, or premium upholstery as the material. These materials ensure that the furniture will endure regular use and keep its charm over time in addition to lending the room a sense of refinement. Purchasing furniture with a sturdy frame and high-quality materials assures that it will retain both its structural integrity and visual attractiveness over time.

Consideration of durability is essential while choosing minimalist furniture. The minimalist aesthetic promotes a space devoid of clutter with only the most necessary furniture elements present. Each item should therefore be able to endure the stresses of daily living. Choose durable furniture, whether it's a sofa, dining table, or storage unit.

In addition to robustness, minimalist furniture places a high priority on craftsmanship. Pay close attention to the joints, finishes, and general construction elements. Furniture that has been expertly built shows the time and effort that went into its production and will last for many years.

The ease of upkeep is another factor that contributes to the quality and longevity of minimalist furniture selections. The same rule applies to furniture upkeep as it does for minimalist decor, which frequently favour tidy, uncluttered areas. To keep the room appearing tidy and organised, seek for furniture with finishes that are simple to clean and maintain.

You may design a minimalist space that emanates refinement and longevity by selecting furniture that is both high-quality and long-lasting. Having fewer, higher-quality things goes hand in hand with the minimalist idea of quality and durability. Each piece of furniture has a personality of its own, providing a function and adding to the overall aesthetic appeal of the room.

Additionally, buying high-quality, long-lasting furniture supports sustainable lifestyles. By selecting durable items that endure a long time, you can reduce waste and the impact on the environment by reducing the need for frequent replacements. Natural materials are frequently prioritised in sustainable furniture designs, such as ethically harvested wood or eco-friendly upholstery, supporting a way of life that values the environment.

Furniture selection for a minimalist design must take into account quality and endurance. The craftsmanship and materials utilised should not be sacrificed for the minimalist furniture's clean and straightforward appearance. By selecting long-lasting furniture, you can be sure that every item will continue to enhance the room's overall utility and visual appeal for many years to come. In addition to extending the usefulness of the minimalist look, purchasing well-made, long-lasting furniture supports sustainable lifestyles. Therefore, to create an environment that is both aesthetically attractive and designed to last, give priority to quality and longevity while furnishing your minimalist home.

Minimalist Lighting and Ambiance

Natural Lighting and Open Spaces in Minimalist Interiors

Open areas and natural sunlight are essential components of minimalist interior design. The idea of a minimalist room is to produce a setting that seems light, airy, and connected to the outside environment. In order to achieve this style, natural lighting is essential, and open areas contribute to the feeling of peace and tranquilly as a whole.

Eliminating unneeded clutter and distractions is one of the fundamental tenets of minimalist design. In addition to lighting up the room, allowing natural light to flood the area also gives it a feeling of openness and purity. An environment with clean lines, simplicity, and subtle details is more visually appealing when lit by natural light, which has a certain quality of its own.

In order to maximise the amount of natural light entering a minimalist area, it's crucial to think about the orientation and placement of windows. To let in lots of sunlight and create a strong link between the inner and outside spaces, large, unobstructed windows or glass doors are frequently used. This blurs the line between indoors and outdoors by letting natural light into the room while also giving views of the surroundings.

Natural lighting has various functional advantages in a minimalist design in addition to the aesthetic benefits. It lessens the need for daytime artificial illumination, saving energy and fostering a more sustainable way of life. In addition to helping to regulate our circadian rhythm and fostering a sense of vigour and optimism, natural light has a positive effect on our wellbeing.

Light-colored walls and reflecting surfaces are frequently used in minimalist designs to increase the impact of natural lighting. In order to maximise the diffusion of light and create a cheery and welcoming ambiance, white or neutral tones are frequently chosen. The natural luminance of the area can also be enhanced by choosing materials with a glossy or reflective surface, such as polished glass or wood.

Another distinguishing feature of minimalist design is open spaces, which add to the overall tranquilly and simplicity. Minimalist interiors foster a sense of space and freedom by removing extraneous boundaries and walls. Open floor plans encourage a sense of unity and enhance functionality by allowing a smooth transition between various regions of the space.

Open areas in minimalist homes also allow for flexible furniture placement and improved natural light use. The elimination of pointless dividers allows for additional furniture placement options and guarantees that the area will remain harmonious and tidy. Open spaces are a prime example of the minimalist philosophy's belief that "less is more," as they foster an atmosphere where each component may be appreciated for its own merits.

In short, open spaces and natural lighting are crucial components of minimalist home design. In addition to illuminating the area, natural light fosters a feeling of openness and connectedness to the outside world. It improves the aesthetic appeal of a minimalist space while fostering health and well-being. On the other side, open areas promote a feeling of freedom, adaptability, and tranquilly. They encourage a clutter-free environment and enable easy movement between various parts of the room. Minimalist interiors seek a harmonic balance between simplicity, functionality, and the beauty of the surrounding natural world by embracing natural lighting and open spaces.

Creating Ambient Lighting for a Serene Atmosphere

WITH PARTICULAR AND with minimalist interiors, ambient lighting is crucial to generating a peaceful mood in any place. The correct lighting can improve the space's ambience by invoking feelings of peace, tranquilly, and serenity. Ambient lighting is essential for fostering a calm and relaxing atmosphere in a minimalist setting, where harmony and simplicity are paramount.

It's crucial to take into account both the general lighting plan and the particular requirements of the area if you want to produce ambient lighting in a minimalist environment.

Here are some key strategies for creating ambient lighting and cultivating a serene atmosphere:

Natural Light: Make the most of natural light first. By leaving windows open or utilising sheer curtains, you can maximise the amount of natural light that enters the room. Natural light offers a gentle, calming quality that improves a space's quiet atmosphere.

Soft and Diffused Light: Select lighting fixtures that emit gentle, diffused light. Stay away from direct, strong lighting that casts shadows and glare. Instead, choose lighting fixtures that have frosted or diffusing components to assist diffuse light and produce a soft glow. Smooth, consistent lighting reduces jarring contrasts and adds to the peaceful atmosphere.

Layered Lighting: To get layered lighting, use a variety of light sources. This entails utilising a mix of wall sconces, floor or table lights, and ceiling lighting. You may create a space that is more balanced and inviting by placing diverse light sources at varied heights and angles. Dimmers can also be placed to change the lighting's intensity as necessary.

Warm Color Temperature: Make your lighting selections from 2700K to 3000K colour temperature light bulbs for the best results. An inviting and soothing ambience is produced by warm white or soft white lighting. Cooler colour temperatures have a tendency to be more energising, which may not be ideal for creating a peaceful environment.

Indirect Lighting: Indirect lighting techniques can be used to provide a soft, ambient glow. Using wall-mounted fixtures that reflect light off the ceiling or walls or hiding light sources behind furniture are two ways to accomplish this. By removing harsh shadows, indirect lighting produces a cosy, inviting ambiance.

Accent Lighting: Include accent lighting to draw attention to particular characteristics or focal areas in the space. This might be a work of art, a sculpture, or a component of a building. Accent lighting enhances the space's depth and visual appeal while preserving a calm atmosphere.

Candlelight: For an added sense of peace, think about using candles. Candles' gentle flickering flames foster a serene and cosy ambiance. To prevent overpowering the area with fragrance, choose unscented candles. Always keep in mind that the purpose of ambient lighting in a minimalist space is to foster a tranquil and relaxing ambiance. You may create an environment that encourages relaxation and tranquilly by embracing natural light, utilising soft and diffused lighting, using layered lighting, and choosing warm colour temperatures. The correct ambient lighting will help you create a pleasant ambiance in your minimalist area, whether you're relaxing after a hard day or taking in a peaceful moment.

Organizing and Decluttering for a Minimalist Space

The KonMari Method and Minimalist Organization

As a minimalist method of organisation, Marie Kondo's KonMari Method has become incredibly popular in recent years. This approach focuses on clearing clutter and setting up one's stuff in a way that brings happiness and fosters a sense of peace and harmony in their home. People can create a neat, minimalist house that reflects their ideals and makes them happy by adhering to the KonMari Method's tenets.

The KonMari Method is based on the principle of preserving those things that make you happy. This entails thoroughly evaluating each item you own and determining whether it actually makes you happy. You may make your space more organised and clutter-free by getting rid of extra items.

To declutter by category rather than by room is one of the foundational principles of the KonMari Method. This entails tackling related objects collectively, such as sentimental goods, clothing, books, papers, and random items. This method of organising and decluttering gives you a greater sense of the number and value of your possessions, enabling you to choose what to keep and what to discard with more awareness.

The KonMari Method's idea of correct folding and storage of goods is another crucial component. Marie Kondo stresses the value of folding clothing so that it can stand upright and be seen clearly. This not only conserves space but also gives things a neat and tidy appearance. A crucial part of minimalist organisation is storing goods in a way that is both practical and aesthetically pleasing.

The KonMari Method encourages people to think about the emotional value of their possessions in addition to decluttering and good storage. Expressing gratitude for objects that have fulfilled their purpose but no longer offer you joy is advised by Marie Kondo. We can let go of these things with thankfulness after realising the part they have played in our life and proceed with a lighter and more deliberate perspective.

The KonMari Method also stresses how crucial it is to regularly keep your home organised. Marie Kondo advises people to make frequent cleaning a habit rather than just decluttering and organising once in a while. This entails setting up time each day to arrange objects in their proper locations and maintain a clutter-free house. You may keep your home modest and well-organized over time by implementing these everyday routines.

There are several advantages to using the KonMari Method and minimalist organisation. First of all, it contributes to the development of a tranquil and harmonious living space. You may create a space that encourages relaxation and mental clarity by purging extra possessions and surrounding yourself only with things that make you happy.

Additionally, less organisation saves time and lowers stress. You spend less time looking for things and dealing with clutter when everything has a home and is simple to find. You can then give your full attention to what matters most to you.

Additionally, minimalism organisation has favourable economical effects. You may prevent amassing unneeded stuff and make long-term financial savings by paying closer attention to your purchases and frequently tidying your home.

In the end, the KonMari Technique and minimalist organisation offer a revolutionary strategy for how we view and relate to our possessions. We may design a basic and peaceful living space that reflects our beliefs and improves our wellbeing by decluttering, organising, and surrounding ourselves only with things that make us happy.

Streamlining Your Belongings and Letting Go

WE FREQUENTLY DISCOVER ourselves surrounded by a surplus of possessions in our contemporary world. Our things, which range from clothing and accessories to literature, technology, and sentimental artefacts, can swiftly swell and fill our living spaces. The idea of simplifying and letting go becomes very important at this point. We can cultivate a sense of freedom, simplicity, and clarity in our life by purposefully going through our possessions and getting rid of everything that doesn't serve us anymore.

In order to streamline our possessions, we must thoroughly evaluate each object we possess and determine its value and purpose. We need to be honest with ourselves and ask crucial questions like, "Does this item make me happy?" Do I frequently utilise it? Does it fit my existing values and way of life? We can better understand our attachment to our stuff and decide what to keep and what to let go of by actively participating in this examination.

We usually form emotional connections and attachments to our possessions, making it difficult to let go of them. But it's crucial to keep in mind that we are not defined by our stuff. True contentment and fulfilment are inside and unrelated to material possessions. Our lives can be made more open to new chances, experiences, and growth if we purge the superfluous things that are clogging them up.

Adopting a minimalist mindset might be beneficial when it comes to streamlining our possessions. The idea of minimalism is to actively choose our stuff to reflect our values and objectives rather than depriving ourselves or living simply. It's about surrounding ourselves with the things that matter most to us and make us happy.

It is advisable to start with one category at a time while simplifying. You may start with apparel and accessories, for instance. Each object should be removed and held in your hands. Do you still fit it? Do you feel secure and at ease when wearing it? It could be time to let it go if not. Items that are still in good shape but are no longer useful to you should be donated or sold.

Other categories, including books, kitchenware, home furnishings, and sentimental items, can be organised using the same method. When choosing books, consider whether you'll read them again or whether they have a special meaning for you. Consider whether you routinely use any kitchen products and whether they are taking up needless space. Choose home decor items that are actually meaningful to you and that contribute to the style and mood you are going for.

It might be particularly difficult to part with treasured belongings. These things frequently have memories and strong emotional connections. But it's crucial to keep in mind that our memories live inside of us, not in tangible things. Select a small number of nostalgic objects that have special importance for you, then throw away the rest. If there are any items you wish to remember but don't need to retain physically, think about snapping photos of them.

It is essential to develop an attitude of thankfulness as you streamline and get rid of things. Thank these things for the part they've played in your life and the lessons they've taught you. Realise that by letting go, you are creating space for future encounters, development, and opportunities.

Streamlining your possessions is a continuous activity rather than a one-time project. Make sure your belongings still reflect your ideals and objectives by periodically reevaluating them. Streamlining and letting go will come naturally to you as you make mindful consumption and deliberate living habits.

It is a revolutionary process that enables you to live a more focused, fulfilling, and clutter-free life to streamline your possessions and let go. You may create a home that truly reflects your beliefs, priorities, and aspirations by weighing each item, developing a minimalist attitude, and showing thanks. By letting go of the unneeded, you may concentrate on what is important and bring freedom, clarity, and simplicity into your life.

Minimalist Decorative Accessories and Artwork

Selecting Simple and Meaningful Decor

The idea of simplicity goes beyond the actual space in the world of minimalist design to include the furniture and accessories we pick to embellish our houses. We may intentionally create a setting that represents our values, fosters a sense of serenity, and encourages intentionality by choosing modest, meaningful decor.

Less is frequently more in minimalist interior design. Minimalist design encourages clear lines, uncluttered surfaces, and a feeling of space rather than stuffing every available space with ornaments. This strategy enables each object to stand out and make a statement on its own.

Prioritising quality above quantity is one of the guiding ideas when choosing minimalist furnishings and accessories. Focus on purchasing a few crucial items that contain personal meaning and match your aesthetic choices rather than amassing a large collection of trinkets and knick-knacks. Choose goods that are well-made, classic, and long-lasting. Purchasing high-quality decor assures longevity while also enhancing the opulence and refinement of your room.

Beyond aesthetics, meaningful design explores the world of symbolism and human connection. Look for items that have sentimental meaning or that make you feel good. These can be handmade objects that have a special place in your heart, family treasures, or souvenirs from your travels. You may give your room a sense of authenticity and build a narrative that represents your individual story by including relevant decor.

Consider the simplicity, usefulness, and intentionality elements of minimalism while making your decor decisions. Choose furnishings with simple, uncluttered designs that enhance the beauty of your room as a whole. Avoid overly ornate or detailed elements that can detract from the harmony and simplicity you're trying to achieve.

In minimalist decor, natural materials can be a big deal. Your home will have a sense of warmth, texture, and natural beauty if you use materials like wood, stone, or natural fibres. These materials have enduring appeal and foster a sense of harmony and balance by connecting people to the natural world.

Additionally, colour is quite important in minimalist design. A minimalist room is built on a foundation of soft, muted colours in a neutral colour scheme. Whites, greys, beige, and earthy tones foster a peaceful environment. Use a small colour palette across your decor choices to emphasise cohesiveness and simplicity while fostering a sense of visual harmony.

The absence of pointless decorations and excessive adornment is another characteristic of minimalist décor. Accept simple shapes and lines in furniture, lighting, and ornamental pieces. Choose designs that are streamlined and sleek and that combine functionality and elegance. Keep in mind that the beauty of minimalist design is found in its subtle simplicity.

By routinely organising and decluttering your home, you can include minimalist features into your decor. Keep surfaces clear of extraneous stuff so that each object can stand out. Display your decor thoughtfully, adding visual appeal and focal points without overcrowding the room.

Trust your gut and stick to your particular style when choosing accessories for your minimalist space. Make decisions that align with your ideals and make you happy. To add your own creative flair and individuality to the mix, feel free to draw inspiration from minimalist design concepts.

A minimalist interior that radiates peace, purpose, and authenticity must have modest, meaningful design. You may create a space that reflects your individual style, promotes a sense of serenity, and adds joy and contentment to your daily living environment by placing a priority on quality, embracing simplicity, including significant objects, and following to minimalist design principles.

Incorporating Minimalist Art and Sculptures in Interiors

ARTWORK AND SCULPTURES are essential components of minimalist home design in order to produce an aesthetically pleasing and peaceful environment. While upholding the fundamental ideas of simplicity and minimalism, you can improve the overall aesthetic appeal of your environment by carefully choosing and incorporating minimalist paintings and sculptures.

Clean lines, simplicity, and an emphasis on the basic components are characteristics of minimalist art. It adheres to the "less is more" maxim by highlighting the beauty of simplicity and omitting superfluous elements. Geometric designs, vivid colours, and a sense of balance and proportion are frequently included in the artwork.

The scale and proportion of the area should be taken into account when introducing minimalist art into your design. Pick a piece of art that fits the wall's or other display space's size and proportions. A huge, eye-catching piece can act as the centrepiece, and you can put lesser pieces together to make a coherent arrangement.

Artwork frequently takes centre stage against neutral or monochromatic backdrops in minimalist interiors. This enables the art to stand out and turn into the space's visual focal point. Pick pieces of art that appeal to your individual tastes and inspire peace and tranquilly. Popular forms of minimalist art include abstract paintings, spare photography, and straightforward line drawings.

Additionally, sculptures are quite important in minimalist interior design since they provide the room dimension, texture, and visual intrigue. Choose sculptures with a minimalist look, smooth surfaces, and crisp lines. Consider elements that complement the minimalist design philosophy, such as metal, glass, or stone. Sculptures can be displayed as single pieces, as part of shelving units, or on pedestals.

Keep in mind that less is more when adding artwork and sculptures to your minimalist space. Keep from packing the area with too many items. Instead, pick a small number of carefully chosen sculptures and paintings that complement the style as a whole and foster a sense of harmony. Ensure that each artwork is displayed in a way that maximises its impact by giving it its own breathing room.

Artwork and sculptures have a number of roles in minimalist interior design, including being sources of inspiration, thought, and reflection. They can arouse feelings, promote dialogue, and give the area a unique feel. Choose sculptures and works of art that have special meaning to you or that make a statement. This will not only improve the aesthetic attractiveness of your interior but also foster a stronger bond between the artwork and the space in which you live.

Pay close attention to lighting when you incorporate minimalist sculptures and art into your environment. A compelling display can be made by accentuating the features of the sculptures and artwork and enhancing their visual effect. To draw attention to certain items and produce a dramatic interplay of light and shadow, use spotlights or directed lighting.

Your interior design gains a layer of visual intrigue, depth, and personal expression when minimalist paintings and sculptures are used. You can make a room that reflects your unique style and exudes tranquilly by choosing sculptures and works of art that adhere to the ideals of simplicity and minimalism. Don't forget to select items that speak to you personally and let them become significant components of your minimalist environment.

Balancing Minimalism with Personal Style

FINDING THE RIGHT HARMONY between simplicity and personal style helps you to design a space that expresses your own personality while adhering to the ideals of minimalism. Although clean lines, neutral hues, and a pared-down design are frequently linked with minimalism, this does not imply that you must forgo your individual preferences and sense of style.

By including carefully chosen items with personal significance, you may strike a balance between minimalism and your own sense of design. The minimalist lifestyle supports decluttering and minimising possessions, but it doesn't require you to get rid of all your personal goods. Select a few standout items that reflect your narrative and bring you delight, such as pictures, works of art, or personal items. These things can act as focus points and give your minimalist environment a unique touch.

Think about using colour while implementing your own sense of style. Even while minimalism frequently favours a neutral colour scheme, you can add splashes of colour that suit your unique style. Use a few accent hues that go well with the overall minimalist style in textiles, accessories, or little decorative accents. This will enable you to add character and brightness to the area without detracting too much from the minimalist approach.

Utilising texture and materials is another method to strike a balance between minimalism and individual style. Although clean, flat surfaces are frequently preferred in minimalism, you can include other textures to create depth and visual appeal. To provide warmth and a pleasing tactile quality to the area, think of using natural materials such as wood, stone, or woven textiles. Within the minimalist framework, these components can represent your individual style and produce a warm and welcoming atmosphere.

A minimalist design also offers the chance to display personal flair through furniture and decor choices. While choosing items, keep simplicity and utility in mind while also considering your taste and preferences. Look for furniture with simple lines and a classic style that will never go out of style. Avoid overly ornate or pointless additions that could compete with the minimalist look.

Personal style can be incorporated into a minimalist design without overcrowding it with furnishings; rather, it can be achieved via careful selection. Pick a few distinctive or striking pieces that reflect your specific taste and personality. Consider making an investment in high-quality items with timeless designs and long-lasting durability. These items will not only showcase your individual flair but also add to the general air of sophistication and refinement in your minimalist space.

In the end, being attentive and mindful in your decisions is the key to striking a balance between minimalism and personal flair. Each piece you add to your room should serve a purpose and enhance the design scheme. Accept decluttering and simplicity while letting carefully chosen furnishings, colours, textures, and materials showcase your individual flair. You may design a room that expresses your distinct personality and celebrates the beauty of minimalism by striking this fine balance.

Incorporating Natural Elements in Minimalist Design

Bringing Nature Indoors with Plants

A great method to improve your minimalist decor and give it vitality, freshness, and a sense of tranquilly is to bring nature indoors by adding plants. In addition to bringing a touch of the outdoors inside, plants have many advantages for your health.

Plants are used as focal points in minimalist interiors to add life and organic beauty. The clean lines and neutral colours of minimalist design are strikingly contrasted by their luxuriant greenery and brilliant colours. Adding plants to your interior will instantly turn it into a peaceful retreat, whether you choose tall statement plants or a variety of smaller potted greens.

Plants are not only beautiful, but they also provide many health advantages. By absorbing carbon dioxide and exhaling oxygen, they improve the quality of the air inside buildings, making it safer to breathe. As a result, the living environment may become cleaner and healthier, enhancing general wellbeing and productivity. Additionally, plants can control humidity levels and lower airborne contaminants, improving the comfort and conduciveness of the environment.

Low-maintenance plant kinds that require less care and attention should be taken into account when selecting plants for your minimalist décor. This adheres to the straightforwardness and comfort that define minimalist life. Look for plants that do well in enclosed spaces, such as pothos, peace lilies, snake plants, or succulents. These plants are perfect for the busy minimalist because of their hardiness and capacity to adapt to various lighting and humidity conditions.

When deciding where to put plants, take into account the natural flow of your room and choose spots where they will add value. Place them in locations that might use some greenery or close to windows. Another excellent choice for enhancing your decor with visual interest and vertical depth is to use hanging plants. To make a pleasing composition that enhances the overall beauty of your minimalist design, experiment with different sizes and heights.

Choose straightforward and sleek pots to retain the minimalist design. Select pots that perfectly match the colour scheme of your house by choosing ones in muted tones or earthy hues. Containers with clear lines in the minimalist style, like ceramic or terracotta pots, can aid in achieving a unified and harmonious appearance. Keep in mind that the objective is to highlight the beauty of the plants themselves rather than filling the area with decorative or too intricate containers.

To include indoor plants into your minimalist interior, you must take care of them. Maintain a consistent watering schedule and offer enough light for optimum growth. To make sure you are giving the best conditions for each plant's health, take the time to learn about its particular requirements. To keep the leaves looking vibrant, regularly dust them and trim any yellowing or dead foliage.

In conclusion, including plants into your minimalist home is a wonderful way to bring nature inside and foster a peaceful and tranquil environment. In addition to improving the aesthetic appeal of your area, plants have several positive health effects. You can appreciate the beauty and serenity of nature while adhering to the minimalist principles of simplicity and ease by selecting low-maintenance types and mindfully incorporating them into your decor.

Natural Materials and Textures for Minimalist Interiors

A WARM AND WELCOMING environment can be achieved in minimalist rooms by using natural materials and textures. You may give your living area depth, visual appeal, and a tranquil atmosphere by embracing the innate beauty of nature.

Think of wood, stone, and organic fibres when considering natural materials. These components enhance the clean lines and simplicity of the design by giving your minimalist space a feeling of organic authenticity. Particularly flexible and adding warmth and personality to any environment is wood. The organic grain and texture of wood lend a classic and beautiful appearance to any surface, including hardwood flooring, wooden furniture, and ornamental accessories.

Think of natural materials like wood, stone, and organic fibres. These elements give your minimalist room a sense of organic authenticity, enhancing the clean lines and simplicity of the design. Wood is particularly adaptable and gives any space warmth and charm. Wood's natural grain and texture provide any surface, such as hardwood floors, wooden furniture, and decorative accents, a timeless and elegant appearance.

Natural fibres like jute, sisal, or bamboo can be used to your minimalist design in addition to wood and stone to improve the texture and tactile sensation. These materials can be utilised for wall coverings, window treatments, and even rugs. Natural fibres' gentle texture and earthy tones produce a warm and welcoming atmosphere that makes your room feel rooted and in tune with nature.

Choose pieces of furniture and décor that highlight the beauty of natural materials. Look for minimalist designs that let the raw textures and grains of the materials take centre stage. Solid wood or naturally finished minimalist furniture can give your interior a sense of authenticity and craftsmanship. The emphasis should be on the natural materials themselves, so avoid overly ornate or intricate decorations.

Take into account the colour scheme of your minimalist interior to keep a unified and harmonious appearance. Warm browns, gentle greys, and muted greens are examples of earthy tones that go well with organic materials and textures. These hues produce a serene atmosphere that is conducive to relaxing and unwinding. They arouse feelings of calmness and tranquilly.

Aim for a harmony between simplicity and the richness of natural materials while designing your environment. Ensure that the layout is open and uncluttered to highlight the natural components. Keep the overall design simple and uncluttered by deliberately using natural materials as focal points or statement pieces.

Last but not least, don't forget to include some natural elements in your minimalist décor. Introduce indoor plants to give your room a touch of life and foliage. In addition to fostering a sense of well-being and a connection to nature, plants also help to enhance air quality.

In conclusion, natural textures and materials are essential for giving minimalist spaces a cosy and welcoming feel. Natural materials like wood, stone, and fibres add an air of authenticity and visual interest to the room. You may create a calming and harmonious atmosphere in your minimalist apartment by choosing furniture, accents, and colour schemes that highlight these natural features. Embrace nature's beauty and allow it to serve as inspiration as you design a room that is both texture-rich and minimalist.

Minimalist Kitchen and Dining Spaces

Streamlined Kitchen Design and Layout for Minimalist Interiors

The kitchen should be created with a minimalist environment in mind, with an emphasis on simplicity, functionality, and clean lines. You may make your kitchen more efficient and aesthetically pleasant by streamlining its layout and design.

Eliminating clutter and extraneous components is one of the main tenets of minimalist kitchen design. Start by clearing up your counters and keeping only the necessities around. The openness and simplicity that will result from this will allow the beauty of the kitchen's design to show through.

Choose streamlined, handle-free designs for your cabinets and storage. This makes cleaning and upkeep simpler and contributes to a neat and smooth image. To complement the minimalist style, choose premium materials with a smooth finish, such as glossy or matte surfaces.

Consider incorporating appliances into the cabinetry to keep everything looking clean. A unified and tidy appearance can be achieved by hiding built-in ovens, microwaves, and refrigerators behind cabinet doors. Additionally, by making the best use of available space, the kitchen design's sleek lines and simplicity are maintained.

Use a neutral colour scheme when choosing colours for your minimalist kitchen. A timeless and beautiful appearance is created with tones of white, grey, and beige. This makes it possible to highlight the kitchen's design and operation rather than its striking colours or patterns. If you want to add some colour, do so subtly and sparingly, perhaps with a few small decorations or a single accent wall.

Another crucial component of a minimalist kitchen design is lighting. To give job lighting where it is needed while leaving the overall room simple, choose recessed or under-cabinet lighting. A minimalist style may be harmed by overly elaborate lighting fixtures. Natural light is also essential, so make the most of your windows and think about installing sheer window treatments to let enough of light into the room.

Give utility and efficiency top priority while designing the kitchen arrangement. Think of the traditional 'work triangle' idea, which arranges the refrigerator, stove and sink in a triangle. This makes moving around and moving along easily when making meals. To guarantee efficient and uninterrupted workflow, keep the area surrounding these important components clear on the countertop.

Keep your kitchen's accessories and utensils to a minimum. Make an investment in high-quality, multipurpose kitchen tools to help you avoid having too much clutter. Group like items together and use drawer dividers or organisers to maintain a tidy and effective storage system.

In conclusion, a minimalist room is distinguished by a streamlined kitchen design. You can design a kitchen environment that is both aesthetically pleasing and incredibly functional by putting an emphasis on simplicity, functionality, and clean lines. Reduce clutter, select handleless cabinetry, and keep your colour scheme neutral. Include effective lighting, and place an emphasis on a layout that encourages effortless mobility and workflow. By following these guidelines, you can design a beautiful and practical minimalist kitchen that serves as the focal point of your minimalist home.

Essential Kitchen Tools for Minimalist Living

WHEN CHOOSING NECESSARY tools and utensils for a minimalist kitchen, it's crucial to give priority to usefulness and efficiency. You may cut down on clutter while making sure you have everything you need to make delectable meals by putting an emphasis on quality and adaptability.

Here are some essential kitchen tools for minimalist living:

Chef's Knife: Purchase a chef's knife of superior quality and versatility. To chop, slice, and dice ingredients precisely, you'll need a sharp, multipurpose knife.

Cutting Board: Pick a cutting board that is sturdy and constructed of eco-friendly materials like bamboo or wood. Choose a size that is appropriate for your needs and the available space in your kitchen.

Mixing Bowls: When not in use, choose a set of nesting mixing bowls that can be conveniently stacked and stored. Choose bowls made of glass or stainless steel because they are long-lasting and simple to clean.

Measuring Cups and Spoons: Measurements must be exact for baking and cooking. Pick a set of measuring spoons and cups that are sturdy, stackable, and easy to read for convenient storage.

Non-Stick Cookware: Invest in a few multifunctional, easy-to-clean non-stick pots and pans of high quality. For greater convenience, look for alternatives with ergonomic handles and lids.

Utensils: Choose a basic set of kitchen tools such a whisk, slotted spoon, spatula, and tongs. Pick utensils made of sturdy materials like silicone or stainless steel.

Baking Sheet and Oven Mitts: For roasting vegetables, baking cookies, and other tasks, a durable baking sheet is required. A set of heat-resistant oven mitts should be included for handling safety.

Blender or Food Processor: Buy a blender or food processor if you like to make sauces, soups, or smoothies. Pick a small, flexible choice that meets your needs.

maintain in mind that the aim of minimalist living is to only maintain what is absolutely required and to minimise clutter. Be sure to choose kitchen utensils that are high-quality, long-lasting, and versatile. Choose equipment that may serve several purposes to cut down on the need for extra gadgets. You may build a practical and clutter-free space that supports your minimalist lifestyle by compiling a set of basic kitchen tools.

Finally, a minimalist kitchen needs a carefully chosen assortment of necessary tools. Invest in high-quality, multifunctional items that emphasise usability, toughness, and space-saving attributes. You may design a simplified and effective kitchen that fits your minimalist lifestyle by concentrating on the necessities.

Minimalist Dining Areas for Intimate Gatherings

THE ART OF CREATING a simple dining space for small parties calls for careful planning. You may design an area that emanates tranquilly and encourages meaningful interactions by embracing the ideals of simplicity, usefulness, and comfort. Focusing on the essentials and eliminating extraneous distractions will help your dining area's inherent beauty to stand out.

Here are some essential elements to consider when crafting a minimalist dining experience for those special moments:

Choose a dining table and chairs that best represent minimalism in the first place. Look for materials that provide a sense of simplicity and elegance, clean lines, and streamlined designs. Glass, metal, or wood can all coexist peacefully in a minimalist setting as long as they preserve an uncluttered appearance. Choose a table size that works with the space you have and can seat the amount of guests you regularly host.

For your dining room, choose a neutral colour scheme to foster a peaceful atmosphere. Whites, greys, and earth tones can completely fill the room, bringing a feeling of subtle refinement and timelessness. These colours create a serene atmosphere that keeps the attention on the guests and the cuisine, which are the real highlights of any party.

Selecting the right lighting may significantly improve the ambiance and mood of your modern eating space. Think of dimmable wall sconces, pendant lights, chandeliers, or other soft, warm lighting options. You may create a welcoming atmosphere that invites guests in and encourages interesting talks by carefully choosing the correct lighting fixtures. Not to mention the value of natural light; if your dining area is fortunate enough to have windows, make the most of them by allowing plenty of sunlight to stream in throughout the day.

Less is more when it comes to table settings. Use fine, minimalist plates and cutlery to embrace simplicity and elegance. Tablecloths in shades of white or other neutrals can give a sense of refinement without taking over the room. You provide a calm scene for the culinary delights that will be savoured by keeping the table settings tidy and uncluttered.

Prioritise useful storage options to preserve the minimalist look. A clutter-free environment can be achieved by hiding eating items on built-in shelves or cabinets. As a result, there is a sense of openness and tranquilly in the dining space. Keep in mind that in the minimalist world, organisation and simplicity go hand in hand.

Think about how you may set up your dining chairs to encourage close-knit interactions and a sense of community. While a cosy area with a bench or a few comfortable seats can be the ideal setting for post-meal talks, circular or oval table forms encourage interaction among guests. The intention is to foster an atmosphere that promotes interaction and deep dialogue.

Pick a few carefully chosen decor items that complement the minimalist atmosphere and reflect your unique style. Choose a piece of art that makes a statement, a vase filled with fresh flowers, or a straightforward centrepiece that gives a touch of visual appeal without taking over the room. Keep in mind that minimalism is about the purposeful selection of significant and effective pieces rather than the lack of design.

Consider incorporating natural materials into your eating space to foster a sense of connection with the outdoors. A little herb garden or indoor plants may give the room life and a peaceful atmosphere. The furniture or flooring can integrate natural textures like wood or stone to create depth and visual attractiveness. You may create an atmosphere that is peaceful and harmonious by appreciating the beauty of nature.

Last but not least, think about the acoustics of your dining space. Create a pleasant and intimate ambiance by using sound-absorbing items, such as wall panels, carpets, or curtains. These additions will lessen echoes, enhancing the dining experience for all patrons.

For small parties, designing a minimalist dining room means going beyond simple practicality. It's about forging relationships, relishing delectable meals, and making memories. You may create a dining room that embodies the very best of minimalism by sticking to the ideals of simplicity, functionality, and comfort. So step back, evaluate your room, and let your minimalist idea to materialise. Prepare to go on a culinary adventure that will nourish both the body and the soul, all while being ensconced in your dining area's understated elegance.

Minimalist Bedrooms and Relaxation Spaces

Creating a Serene and Calming Bedroom

A minimalist decor should prioritise peace, simplicity, and a sense of personal retreat while designing a calm and serene bedroom. By adopting the minimalist mindset, you can create a tranquil haven that encourages unwinding and sound sleep. The secret is to keep your attention on the important things while getting rid of clutter and other distractions.

Here are some essential tips to help you create a serene and calming bedroom in a minimalist style.

Choose a neutral colour scheme for your bedroom first and foremost. The finest colours to choose to create a calming environment are gentle and calming tones like whites, creams, and soft earth tones. The relaxing and tranquillizing effects of these hues are felt mentally. Avoid using loud or flamboyant colours that can disturb the tranquil atmosphere you're attempting to create.

Choose furniture with streamlined, straightforward designs that complement the minimalist style. Pick a bed frame with clean lines, little ornamentation, and an air of simplicity and elegance. A platform bed or a bed frame with a low profile can give the room a feeling of openness and space. Reduce the amount of furniture you have and concentrate only on the necessities, like a bedside table and a cosy chair or bench.

Cleaning up your space is crucial in a minimalist bedroom. Remove extraneous objects and just keep the necessities close at hand. Keep surfaces clean and reduce sight interference. To keep your possessions organised and hidden, make use of clever storage options like built-in shelves or hidden drawers. This makes it possible to have a tidy, uncluttered environment that encourages mental serenity.

The right lighting is essential for a peaceful bedroom. Choose gentle, warm lighting that may be changed to suit your needs and mood. To regulate the brightness and create a cosy ambiance, install dimmer switches. Avoid lighting that is too bright or harsh because it might interfere with relaxation and make it harder to unwind. Use transparent drapes or blinds to let daytime mild sunlight seep into the space as a way to incorporate natural light.

A minimalist bedroom should have plenty of texture since it gives the room depth and visual interest without taking over the room. Use soft cushions, cosy blankets, and plush rugs to add texture to the space. Choose natural materials that are tactile and relaxing, like cotton, linen, or wool. To retain the minimalist style, though, be careful to make the textures straightforward and consistent.

Pay close attention to the little things to create a peaceful and relaxing environment. Make an investment in luxurious bedding that is cosy and inviting. Select natural textiles that are breathable to encourage pleasant sleep. Choose pillows that will properly support your shoulders and neck. Surround yourself with items that give you a sense of comfort and improve the tranquilly in general.

Make use of natural elements in your minimalist bedroom to foster a sense of connection with the outside world. In order to add a touch of greenery and purify the air, think about introducing indoor plants. Use natural elements like wood or stone for accents in the dcor or flooring. These natural components provide the area a sense of balance and anchoring while also encouraging a calm atmosphere.

By designating a space in your bedroom for rest and sleep, you may reduce distractions there. Don't use devices or office supplies that can disturb your quiet atmosphere. Instead, concentrate on making a place that is used only for relaxation, renewal, and introspection. Think of incorporating a relaxing reading nook or a quiet meditation area where you may unwind and find peace.

Last but not least, consider your bedroom's acoustics. Use sound-absorbing furnishings like wall panels, rugs, or curtains to create a calm environment. These upgrades can lessen outside noise and foster a more tranquil setting for sound sleep.

It's crucial to create a place that promotes rest and renewal when designing a tranquil and serene bedroom for a minimalist home. You may create a tranquil refuge that encourages sound sleep and a sense of inner serenity by embracing minimalism, decluttering, adding soft lighting, texture, and natural accents. Remember that creating a calm retreat in your bedroom requires both deliberate design decisions and a minimalist mentality.

Decluttering Your Sleep Environment for Better Rest

TO GET A GOOD NIGHT'S sleep, it's important to create a sleeping environment that encourages rest and relaxation. De-cluttering and organising your sleeping area is one of the best methods to make it more efficient. It can be challenging to get the restorative sleep your body requires when there is clutter since it might evoke feelings of turmoil and interfere with your ability to relax. You may make your bedroom a tranquil and serene atmosphere that facilitates a restful night's sleep by clearing up the clutter.

Here are some tips to help you declutter your sleep environment for better sleep.

Start by going through your bedroom and identifying any items that are unnecessary or don't promote restful sleep. Eliminate any superfluous clutter that has developed over time, such as stacks of books, heaps of clothing, or haphazard items. Keep in mind that the aim is to create an environment that is tidy and clutter-free and encourages relaxing.

Then, concentrate on organising your possessions. Assign specific locations for things like books, electronics, and personal care items. To keep everything organised, make an investment in storage solutions like shelves, baskets, or drawer organisers. In addition to clearing up your area, doing this will make it simpler to locate and get to the things you require.

Pay close attention to your nightstand or bedside table. Just have the necessities around, like a lamp, a book, or a drink of water. Get rid of anything extraneous that can clutter the area and disturb the peace and quiet in your bedroom.

Make sure your bedroom is organised in a way that fosters tranquilly. Furniture should be placed such that it is easy to move about and flow. A large piece of furniture should not be placed next to the bed because it may make the area appear crowded or cluttered. To generate a feeling of space, keep routes free and uncluttered.

Keep your closet clean and organised when it comes to clothing. Regularly purge your closet of everything that doesn't fit or that you don't wear. Reduce clutter and the time it takes to decide what to wear by donating or selling these items.

Reduce the amount of technology in the room where you sleep. Take away any TVs, computers, and other items that can keep you up at night. These devices' blue light emissions make it more difficult to fall asleep and can interfere with your regular sleep-wake cycle. Instead, establish a space devoid of screens that encourages rest and relaxation.

Finally, think about how visual stimuli affect your sleeping environment. Choose a colour scheme that is calming and encourages relaxation, such as soft neutrals or cold tones. Pick bedding and furnishings that promote a serene environment. To preserve a clutter-free and peaceful environment, keep wall art and other decorations to a minimum.

The quality of your sleep can be improved with ease by decluttering your sleeping area. You may encourage relaxation and set the mood for a good night's sleep by providing a tidy, organised, and peaceful environment. Keep in mind that a clutter-free bedroom will result in a clutter-free mind, allowing you to awaken feeling renewed and invigorated.

Spa-Inspired Minimalist Bathrooms

CREATING A SPA-INSPIRED space in your bathroom can make your everyday routine more quiet and relaxing. Adopting minimalist design ideas in your bathroom can result in a fresh, tranquil, and spa-like ambiance that encourages relaxation and renewal.

Here are some tips to create a spa-inspired minimalist bathroom.

Cleaning and organising your bathroom should be your first priority. Countertops, shelves, and cabinets should be cleared of all extraneous things. Only keep what you absolutely need, and find storage options to keep everything organised. You may create a tidy, open area that inspires tranquilly by getting rid of clutter.

Make your bathroom's colour scheme soothing. Calming, gentle colours like white, beige, or pastel tints can be used in interior design. These hues produce a clear and bright backdrop that resembles the tranquil ambiance of a spa. In order to give warmth and texture to the space, think about including natural components such as wood or stone accents.

Spend money on elegant, simple fixtures and fittings. Choose hardware, showerheads, and faucets with streamlined and straightforward designs. For a sleek and modern appearance, choose materials like chrome, brushed nickel, or matte black. Your spa-inspired bathroom will look more stylish as a result of these simple lines and finishes.

Design your bathroom with aspects of nature. Bring in some plants to offer some freshness and greenery. In addition to enhancing air quality, plants also produce a relaxing and peaceful atmosphere. To accentuate the spa-like ambiance, think about using natural materials for accessories like bamboo or rattan.

Bathrobes and fluffy towels can help you feel luxurious and at ease. Select materials that are gentle, absorbent, and match the bathroom's colour scheme in neutral tones. To give them a sense of class and comfort, arrange them neatly on shelves or towel racks.

The right lighting is essential to creating the right atmosphere in a bathroom with a spa theme. To create a cosy and welcoming atmosphere, install dimmable lighting or utilise soft, diffused lighting. To create a cosy and relaxing ambiance, think about lighting candles or putting a dimmer switch.

Last but not least, use sensory components in your bathroom design. Use fragrant bath products, candles, or essential oils to heighten your senses and give yourself a spa-like experience. Lavender, eucalyptus, or chamomile are among the natural, calming scents to choose if you want to speed up the process of relaxation and regeneration.

These suggestions can help you design a spa-inspired minimalist bathroom that encourages tranquilly, relaxation, and a sense of well-being. Every time you enter your bathroom sanctuary, which you've transformed into a luxury and relaxing experience, you'll feel renewed and invigorated.

Minimalist Living Room and Entertainment Spaces

Creating a Cozy and Functional Living Room

The living room serves as the social hub of the house, where friends and family congregate to unwind and catch up. Comfort and practicality both depend on having a comfortable and useful living room. You can make your living room feel cosy and inviting by adding the right components and paying attention to the design details.

Here are some tips to help you create a cozy and functional living room.

Start by choosing attractive and cosy furniture. Select a sofa or sectional with lots of space for sitting and reclining. Choose supple upholstery and luxurious cushions that will tempt you to relax. For more sitting alternatives and variety, think about incorporating accent chairs or ottomans.

A chic and useful entertainment centre or fireplace might serve as the room's centre of attention. This will serve as the room's focal point and serve as a place for family and visitors to congregate. To encourage conversation and promote a welcoming atmosphere, position your furniture around this focal point.

Pay attention to how your living area is lit. To make a welcoming atmosphere, choose a mix of ambient, task, and accent lighting. To create both practical and ambiance lighting, use table lamps, floor lamps, and pendant lights in strategic locations. Dimmers are a terrific feature to allow you to change the lighting settings to suit your needs and your mood.

To increase the room's cosiness and warmth, add plush textiles and warm furnishings. On your sofa or chairs, layer throw pillows and blankets in various textures and hues. To enhance depth and cosiness, choose natural materials like wool or knit fabrics. Include rugs to provide a soft, warm feeling underfoot while defining distinct regions of the living room.

To ensure functionality, take into account the room's layout and flow. Make sure that the furniture is set up such that moving around and having conversations are simple. Make sure there is enough room for traffic to move and that the furniture is arranged to encourage conversation and comfort. If there is room, establish specific locations for certain hobbies, such reading nooks or a game zone.

To make a space seem like home, use important design pieces and personal touches. Display family photos, original artwork, or priceless memories that represent your hobbies and personality. Use natural elements to breathe vitality and freshness into the space, such as potted plants or fresh flowers.

To keep the area functional and pleasant, keep it organised and clear of clutter. To keep things neatly tucked away, use storage options like shelf units, baskets, or built-in cabinets. Reduce clutter as much as possible, and only display things that enhance the look.

You may design a comfortable and useful living room that serves as a warm personal space for entertainment, relaxation, and quality time with loved ones by using the advice in this article. Striking a balance between comfort and style will help you design a room that reflects your particular tastes and exudes a welcoming ambiance. Your living space may be transformed into a refuge of comfort and delight with the appropriate design components and attention to detail.

QUEENS
OF THE STONE AGE

Promoting Mindful and Intentional Entertainment Choices

IT'S SIMPLE TO GET sucked into mindless entertainment in our fast-paced, always-connected society, leaving us feeling drained and detached. However, we understand how important it is to encourage deliberate and thoughtful entertainment choices as proponents of a minimalist lifestyle. We can build a more meaningful and full existence by choosing how we choose to spend our free time.

Focusing on quality rather than quantity is one of the main tenets of minimalism. Not only does this rule apply to our material belongings, but also to the activities we carry out. We can choose to engage in things that nourish our minds, bodies, and souls rather than idly scrolling through social media or binge-watching endless hours of television.

Being conscious of how we spend our time and being deliberate about the activities we do are the first steps towards engaging in mindful entertainment. It involves making decisions that are consistent with our ideals and enhance our general wellbeing. This could entail taking up a brand-new hobby, working on creative projects, or simply spending time with loved ones.

Minimalism pushes us to seek out experiences that improve our lives and leave us with priceless memories when it comes to entertainment. This could entail going to live concerts, touring art galleries, or going on outdoor adventures. Our connection to the world around us can be strengthened and awe and wonder can be fostered by actively seeking out these significant experiences.

Being aware of the content we consume is another part of mindful entertainment. The material we consume, whether it be books, movies, or music, can significantly affect our thoughts, emotions, and general wellbeing. In order to choose content that will inspire, educate, or challenge us, minimalism urges us to be picky. We may foster a more upbeat and cheerful atmosphere by choosing the material we consume.

Our social interactions can also be enjoyable while being mindful. We can decide to participate in meaningful conversations with friends and loved ones rather than idly browsing through our social media feeds. During social gatherings, we can choose to actively participate and be there, fostering deeper connections and lasting memories.

We may savour each moment and completely appreciate the events we partake in by incorporating mindfulness into the entertainment we choose. Even the most straightforward things may be made more enjoyable, meaningful, and fulfilling by slowing down and being present. When we approach our tasks with mindfulness, whether it be cooking a meal, doing yoga, or indulging in a hobby, we are able to access a greater sense of satisfaction and contentment.

It is not our purpose to deny ourselves happiness or to limit our possibilities by encouraging thoughtful and conscientious entertainment choices. It involves making decisions that are consistent with our beliefs, improve our wellbeing, and lead to a life that is more meaningful and fulfilling. We can live more fulfilling and balanced lives by being aware of how we spend our time and actively looking for events that enhance our lives.

Finally, adopting deliberate and thoughtful entertainment choices is a crucial component of leading a minimalist lifestyle. We may develop a more meaningful and full existence by emphasising quality over quantity, being attentive of the content we consume, and partaking in activities that feed our brains and spirits. Let's chose to enjoy entertainment that fosters our happiness, development, and connection.

Designing Outdoor Spaces with Minimalist Style

Creating Tranquil and Minimalist Gardens

Imagine entering a garden that immediately transports you to a refuge where nature's splendour unfolds in its most quiet and uncomplicated form. It's important to cultivate an environment that encourages relaxation, awareness, and a close connection with nature in order to create a peaceful and minimalist garden. This goes beyond just the aesthetics.

A serene, understated garden has simplicity at its core. It's about getting rid of extraneous things, embracing simple designs, and letting nature take centre stage. Start by carefully choosing a small number of plants and items that work well together. To promote calm and unity, choose a restrained colour scheme, such as shades of green, white, and earth tones.

Your garden's layout and design should adhere to the minimalist aesthetic. Take advantage of wide open areas and clear walkways that promote flow and easy mobility. Don't pack the garden too tightly with plants or other ornaments. Instead, concentrate on making a harmonious composition that gives each element room to breathe and have its own unique impact.

The use of natural materials is one of the characteristics of a peaceful garden. To create depth and aesthetic interest, mix in organic textures like worn wood, stone, and gravel. These materials not only convey a timeless quality, but they also provide us a physical connection to nature. To define distinct regions of the garden or to create focal points, use them sparingly and wisely.

An atmosphere of calm is greatly influenced by water features. The tranquillizing effects of the soft sound of rushing water can be felt right away. Think about including a modest cascading waterfall, a reflecting pool, or a minimalist fountain into your landscape design. These components not only provide visual interest but also produce a soothing audio effect that improves the atmosphere overall.

The tranquilly of your garden can also be enhanced with strategic lighting, especially at night. In addition to highlighting important features and paths while keeping a sense of subtlety, soft and warm lighting may produce a cosy and welcoming ambiance. Avoid strong, glaring lights that disturb the tranquilly of the area and choose low-voltage or solar-powered lights that mix in smoothly with the surroundings.

Plants play a major role in a minimalist garden. Pick plants with clear, straightforward forms, including decorative grasses, evergreen shrubs, and expertly manicured trees. Allow each plant to breathe and stand out on its own by embracing the beauty of emptiness. Avoid making arrangements that are too complicated or hectic because they can interfere with the garden's general tranquilly.

A minimalist landscape provides for a more laid-back approach to care. You may spend more time admiring the beauty of the garden by choosing low-maintenance plants and installing effective irrigation systems. Concentrate on developing a self-sustaining ecosystem so that plants can flourish without human interference.

Beyond the aesthetics, a serene, uncluttered landscape promotes contemplation and awareness. Where you may pause, ponder, and really inhabit the present moment, think of including meditation places, private lounging areas, or Zen-inspired rock gardens. These purposefully created areas offer chances for reflection and nature connection.

The process of designing a calm, simple landscape requires careful thought of each component. Finding the right mix between utility, simplicity, and beauty is important. Let your instincts lead you as you set out on your adventure and embrace the minimalist philosophy of letting nature speak for itself. Make your garden a peaceful retreat where you can find comfort, ideas, and a strong sense of connection to nature.

Balancing Nature and Minimalism in Outdoor Living

FINDING THE IDEAL HARMONY between nature and minimalism in the world of outdoor living may provide a beautiful area that honours the beauty of the natural world while keeping the clear lines and simplicity of minimalist design. It involves constructing an outside space that promotes relaxation, fosters connection with nature, and symbolises minimalism's core values.

The use of natural materials is one of the main components in outdoor living that strikes a balance between nature and minimalism. Accept the use of natural textures like wood, stone, and fibres. Choose furnishings and buildings that are aesthetically pleasing and constructed of sustainable resources. This brings everything together and gives nature the chance to shine.

To create a natural and colourful outdoor space, it is essential to incorporate vegetation and plants. Select natural plants that can survive in your environment and just need occasional upkeep. Enjoy the beauty of the outdoors and let the plants develop in their most natural state. Let them take on their natural shape and form rather than over-pruning or over-shaping them.

Careful selection of outdoor furniture and accessories can help to create a sense of harmony and simplicity. Choose simple shapes, little adornment, and colours that blend nicely with the natural environment. Select furniture that fits the room well and is both comfy and functional. Maintaining a minimalist appearance while guaranteeing a comfortable outdoor living experience requires prioritising quality over quantity.

The idea of outdoor living zones is crucial for striking a balance between nature and minimalism. Make zones in your outside space that are specific to particular activities, such dining, relaxing, and entertaining. Maintain an airy, large sense while defining these zones with natural features like pergolas, trellises, or hedges. To create a unified and attractive outdoor environment, one space should flow into the next without any noticeable barriers.

It's crucial to have outdoor lighting that is straightforward and practical. Think about enhancing the room's innate beauty without overwhelming it with soft, warm lighting. Use carefully positioned lighting to draw attention to important details like walkways, seating places, or architectural highlights. Create a cosy and appealing atmosphere so you can continue to take pleasure in the outdoors when the sun goes down.

Additionally important in achieving a harmony between nature and minimalism in outdoor living are water features. Think of adding a simple fountain, a tiny pond, or a water feature that mixes in naturally with the landscape. You feel even more connected to nature thanks to the relaxing addition of trickling water to the environment.

Concentrate on clearing the deck and maintaining it neat to uphold the minimalist look. Accept storage options that effortlessly fit the décor, including outdoor cabinets or benches with hidden storage. This keeps the area tidy and uncluttered, enhancing the beauty of the surrounding natural features.

Incorporate seating areas with unimpeded, comfortable views of the surrounding countryside to further promote a sense of connection with nature. Strategically place seats or chairs to take advantage of picturesque views or to create a comfortable enclave beneath a tree canopy. This fosters a quiet and tranquil environment that enables you to completely appreciate the natural splendour.

Outdoor living is a creative endeavour that calls for careful study of each component to strike a balance between nature and minimalism. It involves designing a setting that welcomes nature while upholding the elegance and simplicity of minimalist architecture. You may create a harmonious outdoor living environment that celebrates the beauty of nature while offering a tranquil escape for relaxation and enjoyment by incorporating natural materials, vegetation, useful furniture, and strategic lighting.

Minimalist Outdoor Furniture and Layouts

THE FURNITURE YOU CHOOSE and the way it is arranged are important factors in creating a minimalist outdoor setting that looks neat and uncluttered. Layouts that are carefully thought out and minimalist outdoor furniture can improve the overall design, encourage relaxation, and foster a peaceful environment.

Minimalism prioritises usefulness and simplicity above all else. Select patio ware with simple lines and little decoration. Pick items that are crafted from durable materials to survive the weather while preserving their stylish appeal. Look for furniture that is both comfortable and attractive to the eye, free of extraneous decorations or cushions.

When choosing outdoor furniture, keep in mind the maxim "less is more". Instead than stuffing the area with a tonne of furniture, concentrate on a few core pieces that do their jobs well. A sleek sofa or a group of contemporary chairs that offer comfort without taking over the room can be used to create a seating area. Accept the concept of open space and give each piece of furniture space to breathe.

Consider natural or neutral materials that will meld perfectly with the outside surroundings. Minimalist furniture made of wood, teak, or metal can give the room a touch of elegance. Avoid using loud colours or elaborate patterns that can detract from the design's simplicity. Choose neutral colours instead, such white, beige, or grey, which promote harmony and cosiness.

The consideration of functionality is a key element of minimalist outdoor furniture. Select furniture with functional characteristics or various uses. Consider choosing a dining table with storage drawers or benches with storage space underneath. This not only makes the most of the available space but also keeps the area looking tidy and uncluttered.

The design of your outdoor space should be straightforward and balanced. Analyse the space's size and shape before thinking about how you wish to use it. Establish separate areas for various activities, such as dining, relaxing, or entertaining. Use furniture placement, rugs, or outdoor flooring materials to define these areas.

By leaving plenty of space between furniture items, you can keep the room feeling open. Avoid cluttering or blocking natural routes with furniture placement. This makes the area feel more inviting and spacious and generates a sense of flow.

Keep the space feeling open by allowing for lots of circulation When positioning your outdoor furniture, take into account the surrounding environment and the surrounding scenery. Placement of seating places should take use of scenic vistas or other prominent features of the surroundings. By placing furniture in line with architectural details or letting the natural contours of the terrain direct the plan, you can create a sense of harmony.

Functional accessories can also be added to improve minimalist outdoor furniture. For instance, a straightforward umbrella or shade structure can offer protection from the sun while also enhancing the design of the area. Outdoor rugs or cushions that are arranged with care can add warmth and comfort without detracting from the minimalist design.

In conclusion, simplicity, utility, and an emphasis on clean lines are characteristics of minimalist outdoor furniture and design. Pick pieces of furniture that are well-made, aesthetically pleasing, and comfy. Design a floor plan that encourages balance and openness, with discrete zones for various activities. Adopt muted hues and organic materials that harmoniously complement the outside world. By adhering to these guidelines, you may design a minimalist outdoor area that encourages rest, nurtures tranquilly, and enables you to completely appreciate the beauty of nature.

Sustainable Living and Minimalism

Minimalism as a Path to Sustainable Living

In the modern world, when materialism and consumerism are on the rise, minimalism has come to be recognised as a potent idea that not only encourages simplicity and decluttering but also offers a way to live sustainably. Making thoughtful decisions that have a good influence on the environment and encouraging us to reevaluate our relationship with material belongings are both encouraged by minimalism.

The fundamental tenet of minimalism is to own and use only that which is essential and adds value to our lives. By adopting a minimalist lifestyle, we change our priorities from acquiring things to valuing relationships, experiences, and personal development. This mentality change automatically lowers our consumption and diminishes our environmental impact.

The minimalism tenet that cleaning our physical spaces is one of its main tenets. We eliminate waste and stop the needless consumption of resources by getting rid of extra possessions that are no longer useful. Minimalism promotes a more sustainable approach to our material belongings by encouraging us to value and maximise what we already have rather than continuously purchasing more things.

Additionally, minimalism teaches us to make thoughtful purchases. We spend the time to think about how our decisions will affect the environment rather than giving in to impulse purchases or the incessant demand for the newest trends. Quality is more important to us than quantity, and we look for durable products that are manufactured sustainably and ethically. This encourages responsible purchasing and lowers the desire for disposable goods and quick fashion, two important causes of environmental deterioration.

Adopting simplicity also helps us consume fewer single-use items and wasteful packaging. We continually look for ways to reduce the garbage we produce as a result of growing awareness of it. To lessen our impact on the escalating plastic trash issue, we might choose reusable alternatives like stainless steel water bottles, cloth shopping bags, and food containers.

Beyond merely material possessions, minimalism encompasses many aspects. It also motivates us to declutter our digital clutter and streamline other areas of our lives, like our calendars. Stress is reduced and time is made available for activities that are consistent with our values when we focus our time and energy on what really matters. This intentional way of life not only enhances our wellbeing but also lowers the amount of resources we use for activities that are not absolutely necessary.

The development of attentive and intentional behaviours is another way minimalism contributes to sustainable living. We are urged by minimalism to consider our impact on the environment and make thoughtful decisions every day. This can involve implementing techniques like composting, recycling, energy and water conservation, and assisting regionally and sustainably run enterprises. These modest activities have the potential to significantly improve the environment when amplified across a broader scale.

The idea that material possessions are the source of happiness and fulfilment is contested by minimalism. It encourages us to reevaluate our beliefs and priorities and look for fulfilment in people, relationships, and experiences rather than in material possessions. We become less likely to participate in the culture of overconsumption and more likely to find contentment in a simpler, more sustainable lifestyle when we remove our sense of identity and self-worth from material items.

Finally, minimalism provides us with a strong route to sustainable life. We may limit our consumption, clean up our physical and digital places, and make environmentally friendly decisions by adopting a minimalist attitude. We are urged by minimalism to embrace simplicity, put quality above quantity, and find fulfilment in experiences rather than things. By minimising waste, saving resources, and preserving the environment, minimalism helps to create a more sustainable future.

Eco-Friendly Materials and Energy-Efficient Design

ECO-FRIENDLY BUILDING materials and energy-efficient design have taken centre stage in the world of architecture and interior design as we strive for a more sustainable future. These creative methods not only lessen our environmental footprint but also produce rooms that are both aesthetically beautiful and practical.

Eco-friendly solutions have become increasingly popular when choosing materials for building and design. Typically, these materials are acquired and produced in a way that minimises environmental damage and encourages sustainable practises. For instance, using bamboo and recycled wood in place of traditional hardwood reduces deforestation and encourages the use of resources that are quickly renewable.

Materials that have been recycled or upcycled are also very important in eco-friendly design. Surfaces, furniture, and accessories made from recycled glass, reclaimed metal, and salvaged wood are distinctive and aesthetically pleasing. These materials not only lessen waste but also provide the entire design personality and a sense of sustainability.

Another crucial component of designing environmentally friendly spaces is energy efficiency. The objective is to reduce energy use and increase the use of renewable energy sources. This can be accomplished using a variety of techniques, including maximising natural lighting and ventilation, including energy-efficient fixtures and appliances, and using solar or geothermal power systems to generate electricity.

Making the most of natural light improves a space's ambience while also being energy-efficient. There is less need for artificial lighting during the day thanks to the abundance of natural light that large windows, skylights, and light tubes provide. A better way to distribute light throughout the area is to use reflecting materials and surfaces that are light in colour.

For designs to be energy-efficient, proper insulation and effective HVAC systems are essential. The need for excessive heating or cooling is reduced by the ability to manage internal temperature provided by well-insulated walls, roofs, and windows. Energy-saving products like LED lighting, smart thermostats, and low-energy refrigerators help to reduce energy consumption even more.

Another important feature of eco-friendly architecture is water saving. Water usage can be decreased by using low-flow toilets, showerheads, and faucets without sacrificing performance. It is also possible to employ rainwater collecting devices to gather and recycle water for irrigation.

Additionally, cutting-edge technologies like smart home automation systems contribute to energy-efficient architecture. Utilising these technologies, users can optimise energy use depending on specific demands while monitoring and controlling energy consumption in real-time. They can automatically change the lighting, heating, and cooling settings, which minimises waste and makes living more sustainably.

The advantages of using eco-friendly materials and energy-efficient design go beyond their positive effects on the environment. These procedures also help to increase occupant comfort and well-being, lower operating costs, and improve indoor air quality. Being ecologically conscious is only one aspect of sustainable design; another is building environments that enhance people's well-being, productivity, and general quality of life.

In conclusion, energy-efficient design and environmentally friendly building materials are crucial to building a more sustainable future. We can dramatically lower our carbon footprint and have a beneficial impact on the environment by choosing products that are ethically sourced, recycled, and employing energy-saving techniques. Additionally, these methods produce visually beautiful and useful spaces that improve tenant well-being. We can build a greener, more sustainable environment for future generations to enjoy by using these novel techniques.

Minimalist Practices for Reducing Environmental Impact

ADOPTING MINIMALIST lifestyles can be a potent method to lessen our impact on the environment in a world where environmental issues are becoming more and more important. Decluttering our physical spaces is only one aspect of minimalism; it also refers to a way of thinking and living that emphasises simplicity, intentionality, and sustainability.

Consumption reduction is one of the main tenets of minimalism. By adopting a minimalist attitude, we increase our awareness of our consumption patterns and strive to only buy things that are actually required. This entails restraining ourselves from making impulsive purchases and carefully weighing the environmental impact of our choices. By investing in strong, long-lasting items that won't quickly end up in landfills, we place a higher priority on quality than quantity.

The belief that "less is more" is a key component of minimalist practises. This holds true for all aspects of our lives, not just material stuff. We may lessen stress and make more time and space for the things that really matter by streamlining our habits, schedules, and obligations. This deliberate approach results in a more sustainable way of life and helps us avoid overconsumption.

Additionally, minimalism inspires us to develop eco-friendly practises. For instance, cutting waste is a major priority. We can make an effort to use fewer single-use items and choose reusable alternatives in their place. For instance, purchasing reusable shopping bags, coffee cups, and water bottles can greatly lessen our dependency on single-use items. Additionally, recycling and composting with awareness can keep a lot of waste out of landfills.

Additionally, living a modest lifestyle encourages energy efficiency. We may make little changes that have a huge impact by being aware of how much energy we use. One can reduce energy usage by utilising energy-efficient appliances, turning off lights and devices when not in use, and improving the insulation in our homes. Our carbon footprint is further reduced by embracing natural lighting and ventilation, which also minimises the demand for artificial lighting and air conditioning.

Another area where minimalist lifestyles might have an impact is transportation. We may lessen our dependency on fossil fuels and lower air pollution by adopting sustainable forms of transportation, such walking, cycling, or taking public transportation. Additional tactics that support more effective and environmentally friendly commuting include carpooling and bundling errands into a single trip.

Another key factor is the foods available. Focusing on high-quality, regionally and seasonally-sourced ingredients is a key component in adopting a minimalist approach to eating. We improve our health, reduce packaging waste, and help local farmers and producers by lowering our dependency on processed and packaged goods.

Finally, minimalism practises can also be applied to our online life. We can make our digital presence more streamlined and effective by cleaning up our digital spaces and organising our files and emails. Getting rid of pointless files and unsubscribing from pointless mailing lists and newsletters minimises our digital footprint and helps ensure more sustainable resource consumption.

In conclusion, practising minimalism gives us a chance to lessen our impact on the environment and live more mindfully. We can make substantial progress towards a more sustainable future by embracing simplicity, mindful consumption, waste reduction, energy conservation, sustainable transportation, mindful eating choices, and simplifying our digital lives. The goal of minimalism is to live in harmony with our ideals and make decisions that benefit the earth and ourselves. It is not about depriving ourselves. We can develop a more balanced and environmentally mindful way of life through these practises.

Tips for Successful Minimalist Design Implementation

Assessing Your Space and Identifying Goals for Minimalist Living

Setting out on a minimalist lifestyle path necessitates a careful examination of your surroundings and a precise determination of your objectives. The basis for a successful and satisfying minimalist living experience will be laid by taking the time to assess your surroundings and comprehend what you intend to accomplish through minimalism.

Start by taking a close examination of your living space. Evaluate the quantity of clutter and extra possessions in each room by looking around. Think about how each place functions and how it fits with your values and way of life. Noticing particularly congested or overpowering areas will help you concentrate your decluttering efforts there. By evaluating your space, you may clearly identify the problems and places that have the potential for improvement.

Once you've evaluated your living situation, it's time to establish your minimalist living objectives. Consider your motivations for choosing the minimalist lifestyle and your goals. Are you looking for peace and quiet in your house? Do you want to free up more time and freedom by getting rid of extra possessions? Do you want to live a more sustainable life because of environmental concerns? Knowing your objectives can help you on your quest to being more minimalist.

Be detailed and reasonable while establishing your goals. Take into account both immediate and long-term goals. Long-term objectives can include maintaining a clutter-free lifestyle and forming lasting habits, while short-term goals might include clearing up a particular room or area within a certain amount of time. You provide yourself a road map for advancement and a feeling of direction in your minimalist endeavours by defining specific, doable goals.

Think about the values that are most important to you when you define your goals. Minimalism is a lifestyle that matches your living space with your values and objectives, not merely the physical act of decluttering. Understanding your beliefs will help you make decisions and design a space that reflects your actual self, whether it's emphasising experiences above material items, encouraging awareness and intentionality, or promoting sustainability.

Keep in mind that each person's path to minimalism is different. It's fine if your space and objectives are different from those of others. Accept your unique minimalist lifestyle philosophy and approach it with passion and an open mind. Recognise that the process of decluttering and simplifying takes time, and practise patience with yourself. Celebrate each accomplishment and recognise the constructive changes that take place along the route.

In conclusion, evaluating your space and setting goals are the first steps towards adopting a minimalist lifestyle. You establish a strong basis for your journey towards minimalism by carefully assessing your surroundings and by comprehending your motives and ambitions. By taking an intentional approach, you may design a space that supports a less complicated, more rewarding lifestyle that is in line with your values. Accept the process, be kind to yourself, and let your goals lead you to a life that is clutter-free and filled with meaning.

Troubleshooting Common Minimalist Design Challenges

THE TERMS "MINIMALIST" and "simplicity" are frequently used interchangeably. To create the ideal minimalist room, however, might present obstacles, just like with any other design aesthetic.

Finding the right balance between simplicity and utility is one of the most frequent difficulties in minimalist design. While minimalism places a strong emphasis on clean lines and a clutter-free atmosphere, it's crucial to make sure the space is still usable and functional for daily activities. Consider implementing hidden storage options that can assist keep necessary goods hidden to overcome this difficulty.

For instance, built-in cupboards or storage benches can offer a location to keep items without detracting from the minimalist design. Focus on choosing furniture and accent items that are functional and add to the space's functionality as well.

The task of generating visual interest without overcrowding a space is another issue in minimalist design. A small colour scheme and a restrained use of patterns and textures are common characteristics of minimalist interiors. Investigate the effectiveness of contrast and layering to overcome this difficulty. To give the room depth and visual appeal, use various tones of the same colour or add subtle textures. Additionally, think about introducing focus points like statement objects or distinctive artwork that give the minimalist space some individuality.

Another vital but problematic component of minimalist design is lighting. The right lighting is crucial for establishing a calm and welcoming ambiance. Striking a balance between utility and aesthetics is crucial, though. Consider maximising windows and employing light-filtering materials to incorporate natural light as much as possible to remedy this issue. Additionally, choose lighting fixtures that are plain and stylish and perfectly complement the overall minimalist style. Avoid using extremely elaborate or decorative lighting, which can take away from the room's simple design and clear lines.

It might be difficult to evoke a sense of warmth and cosiness in a minimalist setting. The cold, sleek appearance that is sometimes associated with the minimalist approach can occasionally feel impersonal or sterile. Focus on incorporating supple textures and warm materials to get beyond this obstacle. To evoke comfort and warmth, use velvety rugs, warm wraps, and tactile textiles. To add a touch of nature and create a relaxing atmosphere, you should also think about using natural components like wood or plants.

Prioritising quality over quantity is one of minimalism's main tenets. When it comes to financial limitations, this can be difficult. High-quality furnishings and materials are frequently more expensive. Consider making an investment in classic pieces that will withstand the test of time and fashion in order to overcome this difficulty. Look for materials with a high level of durability and longevity. Additionally, look into used or vintage furnishings that can give the room personality and uniqueness while staying within your budget.

Last but not least, keeping a space clear of clutter can be a constant issue in minimalist design. Over time, it's simple for things to amass, resulting in a loss of the aesthetic of being tidy and organised. Create a routine of frequently organising and clearing the room to overcome this difficulty. Establish designated storage sites for particular objects and make a commitment to returning items to those locations. Additionally, be aware of your shopping habits and only bring things into your room that complement your minimalist lifestyle and actually serve a purpose.

In conclusion, minimalist design has numerous advantages but also presents a unique set of difficulties. You can overcome these difficulties by addressing them creatively and with a problem-solving mindset. Keep in mind to establish a balance between functionality and simplicity, to add aesthetic appeal through contrast and layering, and to place an emphasis on lighting and cosiness. Keep clutter and organisation in mind while making great purchases of furniture and supplies. With these inventive solutions, you may overcome the difficulties of minimalist design and produce a room that is both beautiful to look at and useful.

Minimalist Interior Examples

Also by Adil Masood Qazi

Writing

Writing Nonfiction and Fiction Book for Beginners

Standalone

Beginners Book of Home Decorating and Interior Design

Interior Styles

Interior Design: An Introduction

Interior Design - A Comprehensive Introduction Guide

Starting an Interior Design Business

Introduction to Entrepreneur Thinking

A Guide To Mastering The Art of Your Thoughts and Emotions

Introduction to Sustainable Interior Design

How Interior Designers Think

Design Your Dream: A Guide to Furniture and Decor Selection

How not to Fail in Business

Ergonomics in Home

How Interior Designers Get Ideas

Ultimate Guide to Understanding Soft Skills for Interior Designers

Introduction to Classic Interior Style

Living with Minimalist Interior Design Style

Living With African Interior Design Style

Printed in the USA
CPSIA information can be obtained
at www.ICGtesting.com
CBHW040728191223
2751CB00005B/346

9 798223 285557